Consciousness
Explained Scientifically
by Substance Dualism

Demonstrates the Existence of the Soul and God

Consciousness
Explained Scientifically
by Substance Dualism

Demonstrates the Existence of the
Soul and God

by

Sanjeev Kumar Jain

www.whitefalconpublishing.com

Consciousness Explained Scientifically by Substance Dualism:
demonstrates the existence of the Soul and God
Sanjeev Kumar Jain

www.whitefalconpublishing.com

The contents of this book have been timestamped on the
Ethereum blockchain as a permanent proof of existence. Scan the
QR code or visit the URL given on the back cover to verify the
blockchain certification for this book.

Requests for permission should be addressed to
sanjeevkumarjain3@gmail.com

ISBN - 978-93-89932-22-5

also available as e-book

Dedicated to the Readers
(Any criticism, comment, suggestion,
opinion or anything befitting to the subject matter
of the book will be highly desirable.)
sanjeevkumarjain3@gmail.com

Contents

Preface xi

1. Introduction - the soul as the driver of life is in
   the Indian psyche 1

2. The mind-body distinction and problems with
   mind-body dualism 4

3. Consciousness: let us define the problem 21

4. Binding problem and mechanism 56

5. Free will 61

6. What maintains the continuity of personal identity? .. 72

7. The altered states of Consciousness -Sleep state,
   Hypnosis, Anaesthesia, Hallucinations, Lucid
   dreams, Meditation 76

8. Near-death experience, Reincarnation,
   Terminal lucidity 101

9. If the brain is necessary for consciousness 114

10. If consciousness is an emergent phenomenon 120

11. Plants are conscious 125

12. Theories of consciousness-Global Workspace
     Theory and Integrated Information Theory 138

13. Placebo effect, Acupuncture, Homeopathy 150

14. Organ transplantation, Cryopreservation,
     Cryptobiosis 158

15. Artificial intelligence and consciousness 168

16. My personal experience for insight 175

17. Explanation about consciousness in terms of
     scientific soul substance 178

18. The origin of life explanation 198

19. Parapsychology and interconnected
     consciousness 210

Preface

Consciousness has been proving an enigmatic mystery. The hard problem of consciousness makes it difficult to explain it justifiably in physicalistic scientific frameworks. If we use quantum principles which may introduce some freedom in physicalism descriptions even then it remains unable to explain our coherent stream of consciousness.

It is presumed by science that life is self-sustaining network of biochemical reaction and all mysteries surrounding life has been adequately explained by science without the requirement of a vital force or divine intervention. And we are just the biological machines in which the intricate machinery of brain neurons and their interactions are producing the magic of consciousness.

Since the 17th century, the times of Rene Descartes, the mind-body problem has been discussed in scientific and philosophical realms but the theory based on substance dualism conceiving the separate mind stuff from the stuff of material body and brain has come to naught because of interaction problems between soul and body.

In India and particularly among Jains, the soul is considered the basic driver of the life and cleansing of the soul from within is required to attain liberation.

So I have grown till mid-age with the notions of the soul but about 19 years back I came to know of interaction problem and why soul is not a good idea in terms of science. I got interested in the subject of consciousness.

In the last two and a half years, I have dug deeper into the subject of consciousness and found that still the consciousness keeps the window open for dualistic terms and for the soul for many mainstream concepts of consciousness.

However, on the back of the mind, the interaction problem kept on pounding my inner mind. I thought in terms of the question of missing ingredient in the conception of life and if this missing ingredient is soul what possibly it could have been doing.

I could feel its presence but was difficult to pinpoint and observe. Then a thought suddenly came into my consciousness from the deep black inside of my brain and I got the solution for mysteries of consciousness and life in sight. Indeed the soul came out to be the driver of life.

Here in this book, I propose the solution to the hard problem of consciousness and free will and associated mysteries of consciousness in terms of substance dualism. I conceive a soul substance different from the physical substance of brain and body, which demonstrably provide a solution to the interaction problem. I also propose the solution to the mysteries around the life and its origin. I also propose solutions for near-death experiences and reincarnations and parapsychology. It demonstrates the existence of God.

I have tried to present the topic of consciousness in easy ordinary terms so that all of us can also understand this consciousness, which is important to all of us.

I want to thank our Jain monks and nuns with whom I got the opportunity to interact and discuss various thoughts and whose blessings have steered me through dark times.

I want to profusely thank internet and Google in particular who made available the material to dig deeper into this subject of consciousness. The book is made possible due to the free and wide availability of the material on websites like Wikipedia and YouTube. I want to thank all those masters whose works I have read and listened on the internet to make this book possible.

I want to tender my thanks to my late parents whose blessings have brought this endeavour to a presentable shape. I want to thank Vinay Alok muni ji and Vigyan Sagar maharaj ji with whom I have interacted on the topic. I want to thank my brother Manoj Jain who gave me valuable ideas and tips for book writing and consolidating. I want to thank Archana ji, Rakesh ji, Kalpana ji, Alok ji, Shalini ji, Dr Ranjan ji who gave encouragement to my efforts. I particularly want to thank Suresh Narang ji who did the type work for the book.

Finally, yet importantly, I want to thank my wife Neelam and my sons Aklank and Niklank for their advice, love and support.

Sanjeev Kumar Jain
January 2020.

Chapter 1

Introduction - the soul as the driver of life is in the Indian psyche

India is a land of gods and goddesses, saints and deities, sages and mystics. In India, there is hardly any person who does not know that he has a soul in his body. The soul is his true self. This soul is a separate entity from the body. This soul is considered as a tiny speck of supreme divine power in us.

The soul is immortal in nature and it departs the person on death. The soul is immaterial in nature, as it neither can be burnt by fire nor can be cut by a sword. Soul merely changes the form and body quite like a person changes his clothes and puts on the new clothes.

According to Jainism, all biological organisms have souls. The soul is the driving force in all living organisms- humans, animals, plants, and microbes. The soul is eternal in nature and exists in the form of human being, any other living being, in heaven or in hell.

The soul is metaphysical and incorporeal in nature but it is the true essence of the self. We have ascribed all the cognitive functions like to see, to know, to feel to the soul. Various worldly sinful activities keep its true nature hidden from us. We have to do good acts, especially devoted to the soul, in order to uncover the true nature of the soul and divine to ourselves.

Because we remain engaged in worldly matters throughout life, we are not able to liberate the soul to meet the supreme divine but rather take rebirth in any of the 84 lakhs forms of life. If we do good acts, only then, we shall be getting rebirth in human form, else may be destined to rebirths in animal forms. Depending upon our charts of works and deeds done in life, our souls may go to heaven or hell after death. After our destined period in heaven and hell, which depends on the sum total of our good or bad deeds in the world, we take rebirth in human or animal form.

This cycle of birth and death goes on until the time the soul becomes liberated. The soul attains *moksha* or liberation only in the human form through the path of *tapa* (self-control and renunciation) and upon liberation, the soul lives permanently in *Siddha Chetra* (the abode of the supreme divine).

Thus, in Indian philosophy, mostly, we have talked about the duality, a duality borne out of different stuff for body and soul.

Most of the religions theorize some sort of substance dualism wherein the beliefs are that immortal souls reside within the bodies and are distinct from the physical bodies.

However, as we shall see in subsequent discussions in the next chapters, conceptualizing soul distinct from the body has difficulties in meeting scientific enquiries and the concept of soul is not a good idea in science.

Then I conceptualize the soul again that is interacting with the body in explaining consciousness and life biology that leads to an explanation for the origin of life also.

Chapter 2

The mind-body distinction and problems with mind-body dualism

Mind-body dualism

Mind-body dualism holds a view that mind or mental phenomenon is non-physical, not explainable in terms of known physical laws and that mind and body are distinct entities.

The mind-body distinction by Rene Descartes

Rene Descartes (1596-1650) was a French philosopher, scientist, and mathematician. He is known as the father of modern philosophy. In 1641, he, in his book 'Meditations' thoughtfully declared that the book is going to demonstrate the existence of God and the distinction of the soul from the body.

Rene Descartes was a rationalist and he based his conclusions that soul and body are different substances and interact with each other by using the method of doubt. He doubted his beliefs systematically which he could doubt based on some logic or reasoning until he was left with what he saw as purely non-doubtable truth.

He said that like Archimedes used to demand one firm and unshakeable point to move the Earth through his lever principle, so was the case with him. He was looking for just one thing, that is certain and unshakeable, then he can build his entire body of knowledge from it.

He conceived that some malicious demon was pulling him in the whirlpool of doubts where nothing looked certain while God was guiding his path to come out of this.

He reasoned that the world around might be delusional, memories could be false beliefs, his own body and senses could deceive him, earth and sky may be fake like nowadays we see a delusional world around in virtual reality tools, yet he existed for certain, amidst all those delusions and deceptions. Then what kind of thing was he?

He reasoned if there was God who was giving him the thought he was then having. He further reasoned if the author of those thoughts could perhaps be him only and there, he got his point of certainty. He declared 'I think, therefore, I am'.

From this point of certainty that he was a thinking thing, he conceived of a distinct soul other than the body. His thinking mind was central to his being, to his existence. He said that mind is an immaterial, non-extended thing while the body is an extended and material thing. According to Descartes, every human being is both a body and a mind or soul. He considered that animals do not have souls. His body and the soul are connected through a mind-body gateway. His correspondence with Elisabeth of Bohemia, Princess Palatine led him to think about mind-body interaction problem.

He wrote about the mind-body interaction in his book 'Passions of the Soul' (1649). According to Descartes, the soul has seat in the pineal gland, which is a small gland, which sits in between the two hemispheres of the brain, and here all our thoughts are formed.

However, later this small pineal gland was discovered to secrete the hormone melatonin, which helps in the sleep-wake cycle of human beings. This pineal gland is found in animals also. Moreover, even when the pineal gland is surgically removed, it does not affect the person's consciousness or mental states or mind. Therefore, the Descartes argument of the pineal gland as the seat of the soul falls flat.

His view that mind and body are distinct, and interact and influence each other is known as Cartesian dualism or substance dualism.

The distinction of psychological and physiological effects by Plato

Descartes often gets the credit for posing the mind-body problem is recent times. However, the problem goes stated since the time of Socrates whose plight in prison is described by Plato in 'Phaedo'. Socrates was undergoing prison term and was awaiting his execution. He felt agony and torture. Socrates dismissed the notion that his plight could be explained in physical terms such as the contraction or relaxation of the muscles. Socrates was recognizing the difference between physiological and psychological causation. This is the mind-body problem.

Intellect is considered immaterial by Aristotle

Aristotle also argued for the immateriality of thought. He argued that the intellect must be immaterial because intellect is not limited in its contents. Eye because of its particular physical nature is sensitive to light but not to sound and the ear is sensitive to sound but not to light. Therefore, if the intellect had been in a physical organ it would have been sensitive only to a restricted range of physical things. However, we can think about all kind of materials and things. Therefore, it follows that it does not have a material organ. Its activity should be essentially immaterial.

Sense of our morality cannot come from the material mind

J. Horgan, an American science journalist says that the mind-body problem is linked to our questions of morality and meaning of life. We make judgments of right and wrong, of fairness out of our sense of morality. Materialistic explanations of consciousness cannot give us moral guidance.

If we are nothing but matter and there is no soul, afterlife, or divine justice we may ask the question of why we should behave with goodness and morality.

What is the purpose of life? What should make life worth living?

Philosopher Owen Flanagan calls it a really hard problem- how to live life in a meaningful way, as we are finite material beings living in a material world.

Soul doctrine is a religious doctrine

Almost all religions believe that there is a soul distinct from the body and which is the essence of human life. Delving and discussing the subject of the soul is the popular pastime topic for many. Many alternative therapies are based on beliefs that power of mind, consciousness, or spirit can heal the person.

Survey on dualistic beliefs

The scientific study of consciousness explores the relationships between mind and body or mainly brain. However, a survey conducted among even highly educated people suggested that dualistic beliefs towards the mind-body relationship were very common.

A survey conducted among the university students of the University of Edinburg, UK by A. Demertzi in 2009 suggested that the majority of them had dualistic attitudes, emphasizing the separateness of mind and brain. They endorsed the existence of a soul that was separate from the body and survived death.

In the same study, another survey was conducted at the University of Liege, Belgium among the people who were attending public or scientific meetings on consciousness and included health care workers and lay public. Even in this survey over a third of health care workers expressed that the mind and the brain were separate and each of us had a soul, which was separate from the body.

These kinds of opinions the people still hold, in spite of increasing claims made by scientists, neuroscientists and philosophers that mind was not separable from the brain. This is because somewhere at the back of their mind, they consider that there is something metaphysical about the mind that transcends the body and brain and they find comfort with the concept of a soul that resides in their bodies.

The advances of science and technology have led to great progress in the field of neuroscience research and have revealed neural correlates for many mental experiences central to human life. In their research study, J.L. Preston and the team of the University of Illinois, USA in 2012 has found a correlation in the explanations provided by neuroscience in the working of the mind and the belief in the soul. They found that people's belief in soul decreased when neuroscience provided strong mechanistic explanations for the mind. However, when the weak mechanistic explanation was provided in neuroscience with explanatory gaps highlighted then that increased the belief in the soul as an alternative explanation for the mind.

Free will criterion

I have free will for certain. Every day, I think of doing something and then do it. If I think of moving my finger, I can move my finger. In physicalist conceptions of mind, free will does not exist. If you claim free will is an illusion or that it does not exist at all, you must explain why I experience it so strongly to exist.

The probing in the existence of free will is an excellent criterion to find the nature of consciousness and mentality.

Vitalism as a belief

Although Descartes gave the idea of substance dualism, he extended the mechanistic explanation of natural phenomenon to the biological systems and held that animals and the human body were 'automata', mechanical devices only.

There had been an idea of vitalism that says that living things were different from non-living because they contained some non-physical element or governed by some sort of non-material vital force.

Creationists believe that life is an intelligent design that came about as divine creation while science concludes that origin and evolution of life happened through natural processes.

Mind-body dualists are certain that there is a soul in the body.

Vitalists argued that biology cannot be explained with this mechanistic view and that matter cannot explain perception, development, or reproduction.

However, as science progressed it was recognized that all biological processes are also bound by the laws of physics and chemistry.

Georg Stahl (1659-1734), a German Philosopher argued that non-living things were stable throughout time while living thing had a tendency to decompose and an agent called anima or soul is responsible for delaying this decomposition of living things. Anima controls all the physical processes in the body through motion. He believed that important motions of the body are the circulation of blood, excretion etc.

Johannes Peter Muller, a German physiologist (1801-1858) proposed that it was the presence of soul that made each organism an indivisible whole. He examined the behaviour of an organism to light and sound waves and it led him to propose that livings possessed a life-energy for which physical laws could never fully account.

Jacob Berzelius, a renowned Swedish chemist in the early nineteenth century said that a regulative vital force was required for the living things to maintain its function. Based on this vitalistic principle it was predicted that organic compounds required living organisms in their manufacture and could not be synthesized from inorganic matter.

However, in 1828, Friedrich Wohler synthesized urea from inorganic materials and later many organic compounds were synthesized in labs from inorganic matter. Miller-Urey experiment made a whole lot of amino acids. Therefore, this vitalism died a natural death.

A prominent 20th century vitalist was Hans Driesch (1867-1941) an eminent German embryologist who held that living things develop by 'entelechy', a substantial entity controlling organic processes.

Similarly, French Philosopher Henri Bergson (1874-1948) coined the term 'élan vital', which translates as an impulse of life or vital force to overcome the resistance of inert matter in the formation of living organisms.

James Tyler Kent, an American practitioner of Homeopathy (1849-1916) says that vital force dominates, rules, and coordinates the human body. The vital force keeps all the parts of the body in harmony and order when in health. All cells or tissues keep their soul and life force within them. The disease is a change in the vital force expressed by the totality of the symptoms.

George Vithoulkas (born 1932), a Greek practitioner of homoeopathy says that there is a spirit-like vital force which enlivens every part of the human organism. This vital force expresses itself as a mechanism of defence against illness. He says that everybody has got a frequency of its own. Homoeopathy drugs operate by the interaction (resonance) of their electromagnetic field with that of the body.

Explanatory gaps in science push us back to some kind of soul

Vitalism may have been out-shined by the advancements of science but explanatory gaps push us back to the thoughts of some kind of soul in our bodies.

There are some thinkers like Simon Blackburn, an English philosopher who think that if there is no magic soup involved in 'being alive' then, certainly, there is no magical thing happening in consciousness. It is simply the product of the brain. The brain itself is creating the magic of consciousness.

Dualistic notions are given as one of the solutions for mystery around consciousness and dualistic soul is also visualized around the life and associated mysteries like its origin and organization.

If it is not showing a selective affinity for organic substances in living bodies and organic substances can be created in the lab even then it must be 'something else' which rules in life. The idea for vitalistic principles or soul for life as such is so compelling felt.

The mechanistic and materialistic concept of life is held with vague affirmation only.

The scientific affirmations about mechanistic concepts of life and seeking details of consciousness in physicalism are nodded by people but with doubts lurking in their mind and hopes in their hearts that maybe, this is not the whole truth or truth is yet to be found.

Science refutes any vital force and physicalism gained prominence

With the advancements in the fields of organic chemistry, biochemistry, and molecular biology no 'vital force' has been discovered. So vitalism is refuted in present times.

Science has made a satisfactory mechanistic explanation for each of the functions of a living cell or organism without invoking a vital force. So the biologists have almost unanimously concluded that vitalism should be abandoned altogether as there is not any requirement of life force for explanations of the functions of life.

The conception of a life force has demised over time and physicalism has gained grounds.

Since the 1980s, an autopoietic conception of life has taken roots, which defines that life is the self-maintaining chemistry of living cells capable of reproducing and maintaining itself. It considers physicalism and Darwinism as its basics.

Therefore, it should be understood that any theory of life force or soul has to be compatible with physicalism and evolution.

Descartes dualism utterly fails to explain how physical and mental entities can interact. This interaction problem thwarts any attempt to formulate any workable dualist theory. It is because of this interaction problem probably, most philosophers and scientists reject dualism and now a day, try to find the explanation of the mind in terms of physicalist theories of mind. The mind is considered just the software written on the hardware of the brain.

Difficulties with substance dualism

How the interaction of immaterial with matter can take place

The basic problem with dualism is of causal interaction. How consciousness (or mind or soul) something totally immaterial can affect something totally material brain (or body). The dualism has come under severe criticism because of the lack of explanation of how the material and immaterial are able to interact.

Substance dualism is most often rejected because it cannot explain the causation of physical events by mental events. It cannot explain how physical actions like walking, talking, and other bodily movements are caused by mental events like thoughts, desires, and feelings.

Interaction means that physical events are causing the mental events and mental events are influencing the physical states of the brain. For interaction, there must be taking place an exchange of force and energy between them. However, science does not find any clue of any such exchange.

However, Interactionism seems to be a natural choice as it states our everyday experiences. The world around me influences my experiences through my senses and these experiences cause me to react behaviourally. My desire to raise my hand causes me to lift my hand and a bodily injury causes an experience of pain in me. My thinking influences my speech and my actions.

Science does not find any seat of consciousness located in the brain or elsewhere. Therefore, it is not determined where the interaction would take place. For example, if someone's finger is pricked with a needle, it causes him pain. As per the science of pain, there happens some chain of events when a finger is pricked. It causes the nerve endings to get stimulated; this stimulation signal is carried through the body nervous system to the brain and a particular part of the brain to get stimulated which results in the sensation of pain. Pain is a mental event, an experiential feeling and so should not be spatially locatable. Pain, at best, happens in the brain but we locate the pain in the finger.

What makes the union of the immaterial soul with the material body?

What is making the union of immaterial mind and material brain possible? How the soul is getting united at the seat of consciousness or at the brain or body? What is keeping their binding permanent because the natures of the immaterial soul and material body are so different?

Closure principle

The closure principle says that only the physical properties of the matter would be affecting the matter. Any interaction of the non-physical mind with the physical brain would lead to the violation of physical laws such as conservation of energy and momentum.

In addition, based on this principle, Leibniz gave the idea of parallelism. According to him, mental causes only have mental effects and physical causes have physical effects. But there exists a pre-established harmony created by God such that it looks as if physical and mental events cause and are caused by one another.

Any action of the non-physical mind on the physical brain and vice-versa would require the application of force and flow of energy between one another.

It has been pointed out many times that there is no logical requirement that only like can cause like or in other words that only things of a similar nature can affect each other. However, such an effect has not been observed and this has not helped in removing the mystery from the mind-body relationship.

Suppose a person decides to walk across the room. His decision to walk is a mental event. This will cause a bunch of neurons to fire in the person's brain which is a physical event and which would result in his walking across the room.

An application of force and an energy flow, howsoever subtle, would be required from the mental realm to the physical realm in causing the neurons to fire. Therefore, this non-physical mind should be making some energy transactions, making these interactions possible.

However, science does not find a hint of such an energy flow.

In a letter to Descartes, Princess Elisabeth said that she accepted from her own experience that the mind did cause the body to move. But the experience by itself did not give any indication of how this happened. She further said that it led her to think that the soul had properties that we did not know, which might overturn his doctrine------ that the soul was not extended ----although extension was not necessary to thought it was not inconsistent with it either.

However, the challenge of interaction is both ways. The question of physical events of the brain causing mental events is as challenging as the mental events causing physical events. However, from our everyday experience we know that a pinprick, a physical event causes the experience of pain, a mental event that may cause us to scream, a physical event. Therefore, the interaction between the mental realm and physical realm is happening within us day in and day out. But the challenge is how.

Homunculus argument

If we remove the soul concept as in Descartes Cartesian Dualism, we need to assume now that sensory data in the process of presentation, is like being projected on a screen in a tiny theatre, called Cartesian theatre by Daniel Dennett, an American philosopher where a hypothetical little person called the homunculus, instead of soul now, is in the physical form, is observing the screen data. Here the homunculus is converting the data into mind. However, how this homunculus is perceiving the data? For this viewing process, another little man inside the head of the first homunculus would have to be present and this second little person would require a third little person in the head of the second person and so on, in an infinite regress.

This argument is obviously flawed. In Cartesian dualism, assuming a supernatural homunculus in the form of soul, that sees, hears, smells and so on, this problem is avoided. Otherwise, we should say that this data or the brain must be aware by itself.

Soul has to have a structure

Even the non-physical soul should have its own structure to make sense of different phenomenal experience fields of seeing, hearing, smell, taste and touch and it would need to be extended in space.

When does the soul enter the body?

Since conception until birth, in the course of development of a human being what seemingly could be the time when an immaterial soul enters the body? Sadhguru, an Indian mystic, when asked about as to when the soul enters the body, replied that he does not consider separate soul entering the body, but it is 84 to 90 days foetus that comes alive.

However, there does not seem any reason or occasion to account for such an assumption. Rather if human beings begin their existence as entirely physical or material entities and since in the course of development nothing like a soul or non-physical outside the domain of the physical is added in the course of development, so we must necessarily be a fully developed material beings only.

If we assume that we are a physical body and non-physical soul then this soul must be present since the beginning. Any theory based on soul should consider this fact.

Ghost in the machine

British Philosopher Gilbert Ryle in his book 'Concept of the Mind' (1949) criticised the Rene Descartes mind-body dualism that every human being has both a body and a soul by calling it as a 'ghost in the machine'. Here the mental activity carries on, in parallel to the physical action but the interaction between mind and brain or body is unknown or at best speculative.

Yet we have an inner voice, which says consciousness is different in stuff and properties from the physical material, which can be observed and measured. So the mind-body dualism in modern thoughts, still have many takers but the mind and the body interaction is yet unsolved and difficulties in conceiving any mind-body interaction lead many philosophers, scientists, psychologists and neuroscientists to deny the existence of any kind of separate stuff other than the body to explain consciousness.

Dualism is not irrational but just out of fashion

American physicist Nick Herbert in his book 'Elemental Mind' (1995) writes, "in this materialistic age, dualists are often accused of smuggling out-moded religious beliefs back into science, of introducing superfluous spiritual forces into biology and on venerating an invisible 'ghost in the machine'. However, our utter ignorance concerning the real origins of human consciousness marks such criticism more a matter of taste than of logical thinking. At this stage of mind science, dualism is not irrational, merely, somewhat unfashionable."

Here in this book, I have tried to present an account that there is a soul in our body that is the source of all phenomenal experience and free will, we have. I have made out a case of the duality of soul and body in terms of substance dualism. I have tried to solve the interaction problem that arises between the non-physical substance of the soul and the physical matter of the body. They are perceptibly continually interacting and we can see that the exchange of force and energy is happening between them.

Chapter 3

Consciousness: let us define the problem

Usage of the term consciousness

If we look at the usage of the word consciousness, we may say like: A person got hurt and became unconscious. After some time he regained consciousness. He became aware of the self and the external world around him.

We lose in sleep and get back when awake

Consciousness is all of that what we lose as we go in dreamless deep sleep in the night and regain back as we awake in the morning.

Consciousness means mental states

Consciousness in simple terms means the mental states. Mental states of perceptions, thinking, understanding, emotions, imagination, memory, intuition, free will, etc.

The problem of explaining consciousness is how mental states which are immaterial in nature and feel are generated out of the physical matter of brain and body.

In terms of the mind-body problem

This problem of consciousness can be defined in a more popular phrase as the mind-body problem, which is about how matter makes mind.

Definition by C. Evans

C. Evans in his 'dictionary of mind, brain, and behaviour' says that consciousness is being aware of oneself as a distinct entity separate from other people or things in one's environment.

How the sensory stimuli are changing into perceptions

Light is some 400-700 nm wavelength of electromagnetic radiation which is reflected from the objects say tree, falls on our eyes and image is formed on the retina. Two slightly different images are formed in two eyes. The light sensations on the retina convert into nerve impulses, which are transmitted through optical nerves to the visual cortex in the brain. There these signals are processed in such a manner that we have distinct, different areas where brightness, colour sensation, motion, shape, orientation, etc. are processed and then these processings combine and we see an object as a whole and this image processing has a quality of 'projectivism'. We see the object as it is in the world at the same place and distance. Similarly, we hear the sound coming from a distance than the self and we raise our heads in the direction of the sound effortlessly.

How the images on retina become experiences of seeing for us? How the different wavelengths of the light create a distinct colour sensation in our experience. We experience dreams and hallucinations where we see mental imagery on a phenomenal screen.

The same is true of other senses. The pressure waves of sound are converted into sound nerve impulses by the cochlea, which are processed in the auditory cortex in the brain and it gives us a perception of 'hearing' the sound. The odour molecules through the odour sensors in the nose create a distinct phenomenon of smell.

How the vision and sound have different phenomenology

Retina and cochlea just act like transducers for light and sound respectively. Brain signals of light after they pass from retina and signals of sound after they pass through the cochlea are the same kind of electrochemical signals. The processing of visual signals and sound signals in the brain, though in different parts of the brain, happening in a very similar manner, in the same code or language of the brain, yet they both are producing the very different phenomenon of 'seeing' and 'hearing'.

We do not know how to account for the different qualitative experiences of the senses. Neuroscience is of no help in explaining how the different sensory signals are getting translated into different phenomenology of these senses. If we knew how these qualitative differences are arising, it would have been easier to find a solution for consciousness.

Colour construct in the brain only

The thing about colour is interesting because the colour is defined in terms of object's surface features, its reflectance, or pigmentation of certain wavelengths only, yet we see a very distinctive construct of colour in our mind's eye. Colour is not inherent in objects. For example, the leaves in the tree are not green but their greenness is being constructed in our brains only. How the colour concepts are being applied to brain processes, is not clear. It is the consciousness where we perceive different colours. The first-person account of seeing colour is the subjective experience or quality of the conscious being. This having of the subjective qualitative experience of the things about himself and the things existing out there in the world around him is consciousness.

Perception and Binding of different sensory signals into unified consciousness

The neural basis of these sensations is helping us to comprehend the problems of these phenomena but there is still no physical theory that can explain our sensory experiences.

Perceptions are not only the conscious experiences of these sensory signals in a passive manner but they are also shaped by one's learning, memory, expectation, and attention.

Perception depends on complex processing of sensory signals in the brain but this processing happens outside our conscious awareness so subjective experiences of our perceptions seem effortless to us. Optical illusions and binding of different sensations processed in the brain at slightly different timings into one coherent experience tell that perception is related to worldly sensations indirectly.

Further, there is a problem with the binding of our sensory experiences. We see the picture on the television screen where we experience the speech at the mouth of the speaker even though we may be hearing the sound through headphones. How the different sensations of vision, sound, touch and so forth get bound in one wholesome experience.

The objective of the scientific study of consciousness is to find out an explanation as to how we are converting sensory data from the world into our experience.

What are the mechanisms that mediate the magical transformation of neural, bio-electrochemical processing into our phenomenal visual and auditory experiences and other sensory experiences?

Finally, we have an embedded 'self' who sees, recognizes, understands and acts upon the visual and other sensory information in our experience.

U.T. Place, an English philosopher says that a physiologist as distinct from a philosopher, finds it difficult to see how consciousness could be a process in the brain; what worries him is not any supposed self-contradiction involved in such an assumption but the apparent impossibility of accounting for the report given by the subject of his conscious processes in terms of the known properties of the central nervous system.

Conceptual formulizations

Views of Thomas Nagel: something it is like to be

In 1974, Thomas Nagel, an American Philosopher wrote an essay "what it is like to be a bat?" in which he made out a case that consciousness cannot be explained in terms of simple materialistic accounts of the mind. He argued that there is something that it feels like to be a particular conscious being. An organism has conscious mental states which are very different from the underlying brain states.

Thomas Nagel while recognizing the difficulties even in the conception of explanation of the physical nature of the mental phenomenon said, "Consciousness is what makes the mind-body problem really intractable. Without consciousness, the mind-body problem would be much less interesting. With consciousness, it seems hopeless".

Nagel was thoroughly unimpressed that materialism could give an all-encompassing account of human experience.

Views of Ned Block: P-consciousness and A-consciousness

Ned Block (1995) distinguished between Phenomenal consciousness or P-consciousness and Access consciousness or A-consciousness.

Phenomenal consciousness consists of our experiences of sensations of seeing, hearing, smelling, feelings of having pain and experiences associated with thoughts, wants and emotions. Cognition, intentionality or properties definable in a computer program are excluded from phenomenal consciousness.

Access consciousness consists of the functional states whereby information in our minds is accessible for verbal reports, reasoning and the control of behaviour.

According to David Chalmers, A-consciousness is the mechanistic concept of brain functions but understanding P-consciousness is the hard problem of consciousness.

Some people consider that mind, in its entirety, can be defined in computation processes and all of consciousness is definable in a computer program and phenomenal consciousness is not a distinct category of conscious states.

Block explains that phenomenal consciousness and access consciousness normally interact but it is possible to have one without the other. Like, he believes that zombies who have physical actions and behaviour quite like us but do not have phenomenal consciousness are possible and a robot could exist that is computationally identical to a person while having no phenomenal consciousness.

One can have a phenomenally conscious experience without registering in access consciousness. For example, all day one has had a slight pain in his leg. He has not paid much attention to it, but it has been there, in the background.

Block shares David Chalmers's belief that to know the source of subjective experiences is the 'hard problem of consciousness'.

Views of David Chalmers: the hard problem of consciousness

In recent times, the problem of consciousness has been formulated by an Australian Philosopher David Chalmers (1995) as a 'hard problem of consciousness'.

The hard problem is contrasted with the easy problems of consciousness. Easy problems of consciousness are relatively easy to explain as they all represent the need of explaining some functionally definable ability, function, or behaviour.

Examples of easy problems related to consciousness are such as explaining how the brain integrates information, discriminates, categorizes and reacts to environmental stimuli, reports mental states or focuses attention.

It is understood that by knowing neural correlates or brain states regarding sensations, thoughts, memory, emotions, behaviours, language and speech and the like, we may be able to explain functionally definable easy problems.

Though knowing the neural correlates or neurobiology corresponding to every ability, function or behaviour is by no means an easy task, yet David Chalmers calls it an 'easy problem' in explaining consciousness.

But all these states of the brain are associated with subjective experiences, the experiences of inner felt state.

The hard problem of consciousness, as formulated by Chalmers (1995), is the problem of explaining how this subjective experience can generate out of the physical, material states of the brain.

According to Chalmers, materialist approaches to consciousness cannot explain why cognitive functions such as perceptions are accompanied by subjective experiences. They cannot account for the felt quality of redness, the sound of music, the smell of garlic, the taste of chocolate, the agony of depression, feelings of embarrassment in a social setting, ecstasy of orgasm. This is the hard problem of consciousness.

Subjective experience means the inner experience of an individual, not accessible to others. It has to be reported by the individual only and relied upon and it is not open to the third person.

Robert Lawrence Kuhn opinion

Robert Lawrence Kuhn an American public intellectual has created a series of videos- 'closer to truth' on YouTube wherein he has presented the scientists and philosophers discussing the consciousness and related issues. He says that the great challenge is to find the explanation of consciousness- the inner experiences of sensations, thoughts, volitions, feelings- the hard problem of consciousness.

Consciousness is a mystery and reflects an insight into our inner selves which keeps the window open to the world of soul and God. So embarking on a journey to search and find an explanation of the ubiquitous but personal world of consciousness is a journey to search and find out the truth and each search and find takes us closer to truth.

The opinion of Edward Witten

American physicist Edward Witten has said that we might never be able to solve the problem of consciousness. Its origination just does not seem to come out of any known physical laws.

The opinion of Thomas Huxley

Thomas Huxley, an English biologist has said, "How it is that anything so remarkable as a state of consciousness comes about as the result of irritating nervous tissue, is just as unaccountable as the appearance of djinn when Aladdin rubbed his lamp."

Alva Noe says the study of mind needs to be richly biological

Alva Noe, an American philosopher says that artificial intelligence and non-biological intelligence cannot have the consciousness in the sense we have because there is something in biological life, the kind of autonomous organization that living beings have, whether they are simple unicellular organisms or highly evolved multicellular organisms like humans; the kind of autonomy and integrity and self-regulation that these living things have that we attribute a mind or meaning or intelligence to them. There seems to be something in the organization of biological systems that cannot be modelled in computational algorithms. We understand many of the life functions in rich details and they have been replicated in mechanical systems but if we want to make progress on the mind, then study of mind needs to be richly biological.

The astonishing hypothesis of Francis Crick

Francis Crick (1994) gave his 'astonishing hypothesis' that, "you, your joys and your sorrows, your memories and your ambitions, your sense of personal identity and free will, are in fact no more than the behaviour of a vast assembly of nerve cells and their associated molecules. You are nothing but a pack of neurons. This hypothesis is so alien to the ideas of most people alive today that it can truly be called astonishing."

The hypothesis is so astonishing because of its reductionist approach. The nature of consciousness, for example, a vivid internal picture of the external world is merely another way of talking about the behaviour of neurons.

He says that the undeniable feeling of free will that it is free will be easier to solve once we solve the problem of consciousness.

Crick reasons that many phenomena in the brain are emergent and, so, consciousness may also be an emergent phenomenon. It may be resulting from a complex brain system that can be understood from the nature and behaviour of its parts and their interactions with each other.

The opinion of Alan Lightman

Alan Lightman an American Physicist says, "For me, consciousness is the most interesting, unsolved problem of science and in fact, we may never know what it is about a particular arrangement of neurons that gives rise to consciousness. Our consciousness, like the air we breathe or like the passage of time, is central to our existence as intelligent beings."

Consciousness will get explained as life got explained- no vital force needed

According to Anil Seth, a British neuroscientist, consciousness also will ultimately be demystified like the life processes have been explained mechanistically. At one time, people proposed mystical solutions like a force of life or élan vital to explain the property of being alive. They considered life could not be explained by physics and chemistry and that life had to be more than just a mechanism. But now, all the life processes like metabolism, reproduction, and homeostasis have been satisfactorily explained in terms of more fundamental sciences of physics and chemistry and any mystery around life has evaporated.

The same thing will happen with consciousness. As we start explaining its properties in terms of neuroscience and physiology, we shall also be able to start solving the seemingly insoluble mystery around consciousness.

Conscious experience as you read it

Consciousness is the experiences that you are experiencing as you are reading this sentence, here and now. You are experiencing your sensory experience of 'seeing' and mental experience of 'understanding' and these are your own subjective experiences. These experiences are central to our existence and make life worth living.

When the child becomes conscious

When does the child become conscious? A child becomes self-conscious at the age of one and a half years or two years. He passes the mirror test of self-consciousness at this age. But consciousness: child seems conscious since the time of birth. Sometimes it is suggested that the baby becomes conscious when he sees the first lights and sounds of the external world as he passes through the birth canal. But a child born through C-section is also conscious. Even preterm babies are also conscious.

However, he gets more and more features of consciousness evolved as he grows. It indicates that consciousness evolves as a feature of connections and reconnections among the neurons. Still, it does not explain how consciousness is generating in the first place.

Animals may be conscious- where should we draw the line

The animal may also be conscious. Several animals like chimpanzees and dolphins show the mirror test of self-consciousness. When chimpanzee looks at the image in the mirror, he knows that it is him only and he tries to rub off the red colour from his forehead. We may think in the manner as to what animals are conscious and why they are conscious. At what point in the animal hierarchy, the line should be drawn such that above it all creatures are conscious and below it, they are not.

However, even the bacteria show the integrated response to the fluctuating environment stimuli. Bacteria are affected by anaesthetics.

Susan Greenfield opinion: Don't know what the solution will look like

Susan Greenfield, a British Scientist asks as to how the water of physical neuro-electrochemical signals of the brain is translating into the wine of phenomenological subjective experience called consciousness. How this subjective experience is coming about from our brains.

She says that not only we do not know the solution but also that we do not know what a solution would look like. We are not able to make any kind of model of consciousness because we do not know how consciousness is getting generated in the brain.

Ray Kurzweil opinion: Computers may become conscious

Even if we are able to make intelligent machines that satisfy the behavioural criterion of intelligence that means behaviourally they show the same intelligence as humans and pass the Turing test, we do not know why they should be conscious.

Ray Kurzweil, an American computer scientist, and futurist says that increasing computational processing and complexity of artificial intelligence will reach one day to singularity when consciousness will just emerge out of enhanced computation and complexity.

However, Anil Seth, a neuroscientist from the UK says, "the prospects for a conscious AI are pretty remote, as consciousness has less to do with pure intelligence and more to do with our nature as living and breathing organisms. Consciousness and intelligence are very different things. You do not have to be smart to suffer but you probably do have to be alive."

Our point about consciousness is not about responses or behaviours, it is about what goes on inside.

Sutherland pessimistic view on consciousness

A pessimistic view is expressed by Stuart Sutherland (1995) in his dictionary of psychology as "Consciousness: The having of perceptions, thoughts, and feelings; awareness. ------- Consciousness is a fascinating but elusive phenomenon; it is impossible to specify what it is, what it does, or why it evolved. Nothing worth reading has been written about it."

Owen Flanagan, an American philosopher wrote in 1992,

"Consciousness exists and it would be a mistake to eliminate talk of it because it names such a multiplicity of things. The right attitude is to deliver the concept from its ghostly past and provide it with a credible naturalistic analysis. It will be our proudest achievement if we can demystify consciousness."

The consciousness of a humanoid robot

A humanoid robot is non-conscious, without conscious experience, it has no inner life to feel. It might appear to behave and perform sophisticated tasks like humans guided by its sensors and computer but it would have no inner experience.

It might detect colours and sounds but it would never know what it was like to see a blue sky or to hear music. It might register when it runs low on energy and move to its charging point automatically but it would not feel hunger. It might know when it is damaged and behave like it is in pain but would never feel real pain. It might act and behave like us but would be essentially dead inside.

The opinion of Colin McGinn

The British philosopher Colin McGinn suggested (1999) that the emergence of consciousness was an event of cosmic significance analogous to Big Bang. Just as Bing Bang created the physical universe so the emergence of consciousness created a new dimension of mental reality.

Consciousness is dependent on the brain

Science has come to a sort of conclusion that consciousness is closely dependent on the brain. Changes in the brain like due to anaesthetics or due to psychedelic drugs affect consciousness. We have found the dependence of every significant mental phenomenon to the functions of the neural system in the brain.

But how does the physical matter of the brain generate consciousness, the experiential feeling, and subjectivity? As Colin McGinn in his book, 'can we solve the mind-body problem?' (1989) puts it, it seems like magic. What makes the bodily organ we call the brain so radically different from other bodily organs, say the kidneys, the body parts without a trace of consciousness? How could the aggregation of millions of individually insentient neurons generate subjective awareness?

A comprehensive description of consciousness

The human brain can easily be said to be the most sophisticated phenomenon that we have been able to observe to date in our universe. And after decades of neuroscience, we still have endless questions about this mysterious structure that brings the world vibrant and alive before us through consciousness.

A scientific formulation of the classic mind-body problem is-'what is the biological basis of consciousness?' This question still troubles the philosophers. When a list of the top unanswered questions in science was prepared, the mind-body problem was at number two. 'What is the relationship between consciousness and biology?' is still an open question which seeks an explanation. Number one question was, 'what is the universe made of?'

The nature of consciousness and the mechanism by which it occurs in the brain are unknown. Consciousness is central to our existence. Our views of reality of the external worlds and our own internal world depend on consciousness. What are the properties of consciousness? What should a science of consciousness try to explain?

A comprehensive description of consciousness seeks the explanation for -

1) Phenomenal characteristics of conscious experiences- phenomenal experiences of sensations of seeing, hearing, smell, taste and touch, experiences of pain and pleasure, thoughts, emotions, inner speech and the like which brings the external and internal world in our awareness. How the physical neuronal firings are converting into descriptive phenomenology. Phenomenal experience of seeing seems to have the quality of projectivism such that we see the things in the environment, as they are, where they are.

2) Subjectivity- only first-person availability of conscious experience. The explanation for subjective experience has been called the 'hard problem of consciousness' by David Chalmers.

3) Sense of self- I or me, the feeling of conscious agency. A continuous state of full awareness about oneself as a distinct entity in relation to the external world. According to Anil Seth, a British neuroscientist, the experience of being a self has many components. There is an experience of body ownership; it is my body that I move. There are sensory experiences like; I see the things where I perceive the world from the first-person point of view. There are emotional experiences of mine, how I feel about something. There are experiences of intention and desire like I want it, I should do it. There

are experiences of action ownership that I being the cause of this action as that is me doing this. There are experiences of my knowledge, my memories, and their continuity, which make me a continuous and distinctive person over time.

4) Phenomenal screen- 'Off-line' conscious scenes appear to be on a mental, phenomenal screen, for example, those experienced during dreaming, visualizations, hallucinations, mental imagery.

5) Free will- free to choose or decide. There is a strong sense of free will in us, a strong feeling of an agency that is free to choose or decide. Free will is a marvellous probe to look into the spectrum of consciousness.

Antonio Damasio, an American neuroscientist, regards feelings as the necessary foundation of subjective conscious experiences.

Binding of sensory experiences in our conscious experiences is another aspect of consciousness that requires explanation.

The problem of consciousness is to find an explanation as to how our sensory experiences, subjectivity, and free will arise from their biological substrate.

For the study of consciousness, we need the scientific study of its subjective as well as objective aspects.

As we probe the material basis of consciousness in the physical substrate of the brain, we find that we do not require assigning new properties to matter for it. Neither, we need to find explanations in quantum physics.

The neurobiological approach of finding the cellular and molecular mechanisms is gradually improving our knowledge about the general concepts of consciousness.

P.Churchland, a Canadian neurophilosopher (2005) says, "Explaining the nature and mechanisms of conscious experience in neurobiological terms seems to be an attainable if yet unattained goal".

However, Chris Carter, an author on parapsychology, writes, "Part of the reason the mind-body relationship has seemed so puzzling for so long because mental phenomena and physical events seem so completely unlike each other. This radical difference in their natures makes it exceedingly difficult to conceptualize the relationship between the two in terms of anything of which we are familiar."

All this time, psychology, physiology, neurobiology, or neurocomputation models have not been able to produce any intelligible model of how biochemical processes could possibly be transferred into conscious experiences.

However, the current predominant scientific view of mind is a physicalist one which assumes that consciousness will eventually be explained by neuroscience and neurobiology but this view is failing to explain why the explanatory difference between the mental and the physical has arisen.

The scale of consciousness level

There are two parameters to determine the scale of consciousness. One is consciousness level (arousal level) and consciousness contents (the composition of a conscious scene). Conscious level is low in brain death and coma and reaches the high end at times of vivid wakefulness.

Generally, conscious contents are more at a higher conscious level. However, the level of arousal is less while conscious contents are more in REM sleep. And the level of arousal is more while conscious contents are low in sleepwalking or seizure cases.

During the General anaesthesia level of consciousness as well as the consciousness contents are low. The level of arousal, as well as conscious contents, is low during the deep sleep stage also.

If any centre of consciousness

Science has pinpointed those parts of the brain that are largely responsible for language, mathematics, specific emotions, vision, hearing and so forth. But we have not been able to find any corresponding part or parts that are responsible for consciousness, the core of what we are? Not only have scientists, despite their best efforts, not been able to locate any brain region for consciousness, but all evidence even points towards this core not existing.

Components of consciousness are distributed all over the cortex and we cannot find any centre of consciousness within the brain. When a patient is given anaesthesia, his neural activity throughout the brain shuts down uniformly.

It seems in our brains roughly 86 billion neurons all act by themselves and communicate with one another without any central agency. Our consciousness is being generated from this biological computer called the brain without a CPU.

In our quest for finding some sort of what we are, if we look in the basic building blocks, the biomolecules and further deep to the atoms and molecules they are made of, in the neurons, we fail to find any trace of any kind of soul or any other clue for consciousness.

However, if no specific region of the brain, or the neurons, or the building blocks that our neurons consist of, can account for the phenomenon of our consciousness then what is it that makes us conscious? What is the current scientific assessment as to what brings it about?

The predominant view among neuroscientists today is that the brain alone creates conscious experience. The brain is described as a genetically programmed computer who's electrical and biochemical processes produce what we experience as thought and decision-making. Although some scientific literature acknowledges that the question is still open.

It is, therefore, no surprise that science headlines today suggest that the experience of free will is merely an illusion, a by-product of so-called background noise in the brain.

However, some acclaimed scientists like Bruce Greyson, an NDE researcher from the University of Virginia, present a very different picture. The evidence he presents suggests that the brain alone does not produce consciousness but rather the source and locus of consciousness is non-material.

Neuroimaging studies are helping in studies of neuroscience

Neuroscience is increasingly using neuroimaging technologies to consider links between specific brain states and conscious experiences.

Structural imaging shows the brain's anatomy and is useful in identifying large-scale tumours, diseases, and injuries while functional imaging shows the metabolic activities in the brain, like blood flow, to let us observe correlations between specific mental functions and activity in particular brain areas.

Philosophical and scientific theories of consciousness

There have been many philosophical and scientific theories to explore the biological basis of consciousness.

Firstly, there are two schools of thoughts where consciousness and mental states are reducible or irreducible to brain states-

Reductionists- Reductionists suggest that particular mental events are identical to particular neural events. The nature and mechanisms of conscious experiences will eventually be explained by neuroscience in toto. Philosopher Daniel Dennett is the leading proponent of reductionism.

Non-reductionists- Non-reductionists suggest that although mental properties depend on the physical brain states they are not reducible to them. Experience cannot be described in physical terms. Leading proponents are David Chalmers and John Searle.

Conceptually, there are many kinds of theories which provide perspectives in explaining consciousness-

Physicalism or materialism

Materialists consider that the brain, the physical material, is producing consciousness. They do not consider that anything non- physical or soul can be remotely accounted for consciousness. For them, the brain is the de-facto organ of producing consciousness and the materiality of the brain is not in doubt. And this is the problem of consciousness. How can a physical brain with all its electrochemical properties of the neurons give rise to subjective experiences of our consciousness- experiences of sensory perceptions, pain, feelings, thoughts, desires, and emotions? This is called the hard problem of consciousness by David Chalmers in1995.

According to him, we can conceive of functional/ computational properties that can be made into artificial intelligence and robotics-based machines and properties definable in a computer program would remain an easy problem of consciousness as contrasted to the property of subjective experience of consciousness.

Reductive physicalist like Daniel Dennett and Marvin Minsky considers that there is no hard problem. The hard problem itself will be functionally definable in terms of easy problems and it will be solved in the process of answering the so-called easy solvable problems. So they consider that consciousness will be reduced down to its physical or material basis. Physicalism is the same as materialism.

But consciousness has the peculiar characteristic of subjectivity. The material world is open to a third-person account. So it will require a real explanation as to how subjectivity arises from the material things.

Physical processes, no matter how complex should have objective properties. You cannot combine objective matter and its objective properties like forces and fields in any manner such that invisible subjective emerges out of it. It would be difficult to understand that something unobservable is emerging out of observables.

Philosophically there had been the ideas within the parameters of physicalism mainly behaviourism and functionalism to explain the problem of consciousness-

Behaviourism

Behaviourists claim that only behaviours and actions are of practical importance and they did away with consciousness altogether. But this concept is frivolous. A person may be doing acting only of pain but there is no conscious experience of pain.

John Watson, a behaviourist, wrote (1972), "Behaviourism claims that consciousness is neither a definite nor a usable concept. The behaviourist, who has been trained always as an experimentalist, holds further, that belief in the existence of consciousness goes back to the ancient days of superstition and magic."

Functionalism

Functionalists have suggested that brain states interact with one another to affect behaviour. Here brains are physical machines made in the neural substrate and its mental states are identified by the function they do rather than what they are made of. Identity of mental state (like thought, desire, being in pain, etc.) is to be determined by the causal relation it has with sensory inputs, other mental states, and behaviour.

This deals with causal relationships and ignores the phenomenal and the experiential or 'felt' aspect of mind.

For a functionalist, since mental states are identifiable by their functional role, so they are realizable even in computers if that system performs the appropriate functions.

Hilary Putnam was a major proponent of functionalism. Other philosophical ideas to elaborate on the nature of consciousness are discussed here-

Epiphenomenalism

Epiphenomenalism is the view that mental events are caused by the physical substrate of the brain but mental events have no effect upon physical events. It is just a useless epiphenomenon, by-product of the underlying brain states.

Causal closure principle of the physical world suggests that physical events should have a physical reason, cause; which then suggests that the mental realm can not affect the physical realm so conscious experiences may be 'epiphenomenal', a useless

by-product associated with brain states and could in principle be done without.

In 1874, Thomas Huxley argued that consciousness is a mere epiphenomenon of particular physical interactions. Today such issues are sometimes discussed using thought experiments involving philosophical zombies, hypothetical entities that look and act like humans but lack consciousness. For example, one may ask if both zombies and humans are reducible to computations or algorithms running on the human body appearing hardware. Indeed many assume that human behaviour and consciousness may be explainable in a mechanical, computable kind of way.

Non-reductive functionalists such as Chalmers (1995) who claim that functional properties of the brain give rise to consciousness, but they are not identical with conscious experiences, they often endorse epiphenomenalism: brain activity gives rise to conscious experiences but since the physical realm is causally closed, conscious experiences themselves have no causal consequences.

The question can still be raised as to how the physical stuff of the brain is producing these epiphenomenal mind states.

Epiphenomenalism and physicalism implications pose a difficult problem for the experiences of free will.

Dualism

According to Cartesian dualism, consciousness exists in a non-physical mode, different from the physical stuff of the underlying brain. Mind stuff and brain stuff are two different kinds of things interacting with each other.

The interaction problem between the mind and body thwarts away attempt to build a workable dualist theory. Probably, because of such intractable problems with dualism, most philosophers and scientists reject dualism in favour of physicalism or materialism or naturalism.

Rene Descartes (1641) proposed his theory of Cartesian dualism which failed on interaction criterion miserably. However, it has brought the mind-body problem in the scientific realm which calls for a solution.

In present times, the dominant view is that neurobiology will be able to explain consciousness without the non-physical stuff.

The dualistic formulation of the mind-body problem in which consciousness arises from the non-material soul has failed to produce a scientific theory.

Interactionism

Any theory of consciousness has to take up the question of whether conscious experiences have causal effects in the physical world.

Common sense observations tell that mental states have causal effects in the physical world but it seems contrary to science to suggest non-physical causes for physical events.

Interactionism is the idea that mental events influence the brain states and brain states cause the mental states i.e. they interact causally with one another.

Parallelism

There is an idea of parallelism proposed by Leibniz to solve out the principle of causal closure. He proposed that mental events are caused by mind and the physical events are caused by physical matter and they run parallelly and so harmoniously due to pre-established harmony set in place by God such that they give a feel that mental events are causing physical events and vice-versa.

Searle's biological naturalism

John Searle dubs his view as 'biological naturalism' (1992). He says, "The mystery of consciousness today is in roughly the same shape that the mystery of life was before the development of molecular biology or the mystery of electromagnetism was before Clerk Maxwell equations. It seems mysterious because we do not know how the system of neurophysiology to consciousness works and an adequate knowledge of how it works would remove the mystery."

He says that consciousness is real and cannot be reduced to something else. It is causally related to the state of the brain. The brain has special, right causal powers that are attributed to the biochemistry of the human brain. The physical substrate of the biological brain is important for consciousness to happen. Consciousness is caused by neurobiological processes and is as much a part of the natural biological order as other biological features such as photosynthesis, digestion, or mitosis.

Because we do not know how the brain is producing consciousness so, we are not in a position to know how to do it artificially.

Panpsychism

Panpsychism is a concept that all matter is conscious. Panpsychists claim that human consciousness is resulting when these basic matter components with mentality are arranging themselves in complex patterns.

One such panpsychism theory proposed by Hameroff and Penrose (1996) is their ORCH-OR theory wherein they proposed that quantum gravity induced wave function collapses in space-time called objective reduction cause proto-conscious events in the universe. Biology has evolved a mechanism to orchestrate such events and to couple them to neuronal activity resulting in conscious moments and thence also to causal control of behaviour.

According to the theory, coherent quantum processes in microtubules in neurons result in the objective reduction, producing conscious events having experiential qualities.

However, it is pointed out that wet, warm and noisy environment in the body cannot hold the quantum processes in the microtubules.

If we assume proto-consciousness in all matter, even then phenomenal consciousness is difficult to explain because of a combination problem, that is, how these elemental conscious elements could have combined to produce our conscious experiences.

Idealism

Idealists consider the consciousness to be fundamental and the physical objective world as illusion or themselves conscious. The main argument for idealism is that physical properties and physical knowledge of the material objects are reducible into and derived from experiences.

The theory of conscious agents by Donald Hoffman is one such idealism theory. It presumes that consciousness creates brain activity, and indeed creates all objects and properties of the physical world. For a conscious realist, perceptions that are species-specific are like window interface where space-time is a species-specific desktop and physical objects are like icons thereon of conscious agents. Here consciousness is fundamental while the matter is derivative.

Idealism advocates that consciousness is all that exists, the material world and science is an illusion which is difficult to accept. The physical world is taken to be objective in the sense that it does not depend on the perceiver for its existence.

Mysterianism

A philosophical position that the problem of consciousness cannot be resolved by humans is called mysterianism.

American philosopher, Colin McGinn is a mysterian as he argues that humans are cognitively closed to solve the problem of consciousness. Like a monkey can never read the newspaper, similarly, for humans, consciousness is a mystery, they will never unravel.

Mysterians avoid dualism. They do not believe in anything supernatural or divine or soul. They are however non-reductive physicalists that subjective experiential feeling is for real and is not reducible to physical brain matter but it is somehow getting made out of the brain matter itself.

They just opine that the human mind lacks the capacity of bridging the explanatory gap between mind and brain.

However, the main opposition to this theory claims that historically human mind has proved its ability to find solutions for difficult problems of our world through scientific endeavours and it will be able to unravel the mystery of consciousness also.

Scientific theories of consciousness

Scientific theories of consciousness are based on neurobiological mechanisms which describe anatomical or physiological features for conscious experiences. Some are based on information processing features of the brain. Many scientists have proposed discreet theories that speak as to which neural activities or which functional relations may be giving rise to our experiences in consciousness.

Crick and Koch (1990) proposed that high frequency (around 40 Hz) neural oscillations in the cerebral cortex are the biological basis of consciousness.

Crick and Koch (2005) have also proposed that the Claustrum, which is a thin, irregular, sheet-like neuronal structure, seating underneath the inner surface of the neocortex, may be responsible for the integrated nature of conscious experience.

Baars (1988) proposed that consciousness arises from the contents of a global workspace, a sort of broadcast of the dominant content from among the various unconscious processes over the widespread area of the brain.

Edelman and Tononi (2000) proposed that consciousness is generated from the interactions of neurons connected in re-entrant architecture in the brain.

Hameroff and Penrose (1996) proposed that the collapse of quantum processes in the microtubules give rise to consciousness.

Donald Hoffman (2008) proposed that consciousness is fundamental and it creates the reality of physical objects in our perceptions.

These theories, however, have not been able to explain consciousness, acceptable to the scientific community but they do indicate the efforts of scientists and philosophers in explaining consciousness.

Neural correlates of consciousness

The phenomenon of consciousness is a robust thing which calls for explanation. Consciousness gets intimately correlated to the activity of the brain and it has an important influence on behaviour.

Neural correlates are the correlations between brain regions or groups of neurons and our conscious experiences.

The researches in neuroscience have found that every well-studied mental phenomenon gets correlated to the neural system of physical brain substrate. Such correlations convince most researchers that brain activity gives rise to or is somehow the basis for consciousness.

Edelman (2004) says, "There is now a vast amount of empirical evidence to support the idea that consciousness emerges from the organization and operation of the brain".

Similarly, Koch (2004) argues, "The fundamental question at the heart of the mind-body problem is, what is the relation between the conscious mind and the electrochemical interactions in the body that give rise to it? How do conscious experiences emerge from the network of the neurons?"

Colin McGinn also calls the brain a de-facto basis of consciousness.

The research for neural correlates has found that consciousness largely depends on the brain stem and thalamus for arousal and recurrent electrical activity between the cortex and the thalamus at gamma-band frequencies for awareness. This thalamocortical network forms the final path of the sleep/wake mechanism also.

Consciousness makes us aware of our existence

Consciousness is arguably the most important thing for us, yet science cannot explain it. As we know more and more of the neural correlates of consciousness, we shall know more of how the physical brain substrate states are making the experience of consciousness for us. But the hard problem of subjectivity will require a real out of the box explanation as any explanation in terms of physical processes or algorithms will not suffice for subjectivity.

If consciousness is real, then scientific materialism, physicalism is quite inadequate. The only way to hang on to physicalism is to say that consciousness is an illusion like Daniel Dennett. Personally, I cannot do that; like Descartes, the one thing I cannot doubt is that I am aware of some kind of existence. Without consciousness, there might as well as be nothing rather than something.

Chapter 4

Binding problem and mechanism

Binding problem

The Binding Problem is a problem whose answer is yet to be found, as there is no well-accepted theory or model in the physical substrate of the brain as to how the different features encoded in different brain modules are combined for our unified perception, decision, and action.

When we see an object, we see its colour, shape, motion, sound etc. All these features of the object are interpreted by the different, specialized set of neurons in the brain. However, we have a unity of experience of that object. All these separate processing of these different characteristics of the same object get bound and we get an experience of that object as one. How the binding of the different phenomenon of the same object so as to give the unity of its experience is being made out in the brain is still not understandable in neuroscience.

Different sensory inputs not only are processed in different brain regions but also at slightly different times and yet are bound together into unified conscious content. How our conscious contents get bound into unified percepts?

Neurobiological studies demonstrate that different cortical areas show increased neural activity in response to different features of the visual stimulus like colour, shape, and motion. Many studies have suggested that perception of different features like colour, shape, size, location, or motion can be uniquely disrupted without disrupting others due to damage to different areas of the brain. These observations present us the binding problem as to what mechanisms bind these features together to give us a unified perception, as we find no individual or small group of neurons that have unified understanding.

This is called the second binding problem (BP2) or the combination problem.

Firstly, there is a segregation problem, which is often called binding problem number 1 (BP1). How the complex patterns of sensory inputs are separated out and are allocated to different specialized parts of the brain. When a picture containing a yellow square and a blue circle is viewed, some neurons signal in response to yellow, others in response to blue, still others to a square shape or a circle shape. Here the BP1 is the issue of how the brain is allocating to the different set of neurons so that pairing of colour and shape is maintained so that yellow goes with square and blue with the circle only.

Binding mechanism

Gamma activity as a binding mechanism: - One hypothesis suggests that features of an individual object are bound or segregated via 40 Hz gamma range oscillations in neuronal potentials.

Gamma activity and its synchronisation over far-out regions of the brain have long been explored for a possible role in consciousness for its theory of binding mechanisms for sensory awareness.

Work by Rodriguez and team in 1999 suggested that long-range synchronization of 40HZ (30-80HZ gamma oscillations) activity followed by rapid desynchronization could be the solution to the problem of how the brain can effectively integrate the activity of discrete neuronal modules to form a unified experience of the world.

In their experiment, they recorded electrical brain activity from subjects while they perceived ambiguous visual stimuli, either faces or meaningless shapes. They found that only face perception induced a long-distance pattern of synchronization, corresponding to the moment of perception itself. Then there happened a period of strong desynchronisation which marked the transition between the moment of perception and the ensuing motor response. The researchers suggested that this desynchronization reflected a process where active uncoupling of the underlying neural ensembles took place and that was necessary to proceed from one cognitive state to another.

However, further studies have found that 40 Hz activity persisted even during anaesthetized states suggesting that it is not sufficient to sustain consciousness. Although persistent synchrony of gamma during anaesthesia is distinct from precise, stimulus-related temporal coordination, which appears consistent with effective information transfer required for normal consciousness, yet 40HZ gamma has fallen out of favour as a correlate of consciousness.

40HZ oscillation of gamma activity is not indicative of cognitive function rather it generates when neuron activates for any of its reasons and when its excitation is balanced with inhibition. As such, these gamma oscillations would appear during a variety of neural control operations that enable neural tissue to perform its system-level functions but they do not perform those functions themselves. As correlates of neural activations, gamma activity covaries with cognitive activity and this has led to their association with 'binding with synchrony'.

Feature Integration Theory: - Feature Integration Theory of Treisman suggested that binding between features is accomplished through common location tags. Anne Treisman's Feature Integration Theory (1980) says that for each feature such as colour and shape, there is a feature map that indicates the location of each instance of the feature in the visual field. Therefore, every instantiation of the feature contains the feature identity and location. Binding happens when attention is paid to a particular location. The neurons corresponding to this location in each feature map get active excluding those neurons of other locations and all the features of the same location get bound.

Evidence for this theory comes from experiments that show when scanty attention is paid to the object, illusory conjunctions of the features may occur in various situations. Support for this theory also comes from Balint's syndrome patients who are unable to focus attention on individual objects. If presented with simple stimuli such as a 'blue O' or 'red T', in 23% trails they report seeing 'red O' or a 'blue T'.

Binding problem is to find an explanation as to how the brain mechanisms construct the phenomenal experience of the object. The statement of the problem can be put as to 'how sensory data segregates into, different component signals for specialized brain modules when a picture containing, for instance, 'yellow square' and 'blue circle' is viewed and then recombines them into a single phenomenal experience of a yellow square next to a blue circle plus all other features of their context'.

Any theory seeking to explain consciousness should also address to this binding problem of consciousness features.

Chapter 5

Free will

There are popular prediction makers who either by hand readings or by horoscope readings can predict future events in one's life. However, there had been a study spread over 20 years, where the movements of planets or planet positions at the time of one's birthday and time do not determine the course of his life at all.

If I want to raise my arm, I can. I make a decision and I raise my arm. It is my free will.

However, our bodies are just the ensemble of physical matter amenable to all well laid out physical laws. Here everything is deterministic. Any future event is determined by past events. Our actions are deterministic to all extents.

However, we have a compelling sense of causation and free will. We feel that these were our decisions. I made this action of raising my arm of my own volition.

In fact, we having free will is one of the main dimensions of the problem of consciousness.

If my mental activity, my consciousness is going to be meaningful at all it has to cause something and something has to be the result of it, otherwise it will be just like fluffy froth floating away on the wave. How the concept of mental causation can be viewed in scientific terms.

If we follow the closure principle where only physical causes can trigger the physical events according to the physical laws, we have to consider mental events as some sort of epiphenomenal or non-causal for physical events. Moreover, the world will be entirely deterministic which means that there should be only one possible future at any given moment and you should be able to predict that.

If we take into account the indeterminism introduced into the system due to noise then things may appear to be happening by chance or randomly but in fact, they very well seem to be happening as per our thoughts and mental activity and not random.

Many of us have the first thought that our thoughts and actions are free.

In our societal and legal structure, the people are held responsible for their actions because they are understood to have made good or bad choices.

However, we also believe by science principles that every effect has a cause. Everything that happens in present is the result of events that happened in the past.

The view that all events are caused by past events such that nothing other than what does happen, could happen, is known as **hard determinism**.

The view that humans have the capacity to make choices which are not determined by past events; they are capable of entirely free actions of their own choice is known as **libertarian free will**.

Although the physical world is deterministic and any physical event is caused by a previous physical event, yet having a free will means that humans have a causal mental agency, which can start the chain of events by itself.

On the capacity of humans of having a causal mental agency the views of the philosophers vary. They ask, where will those free decisions, which can start an entirely new chain of events, come from?

Suppose I decide to move across the room. My desire, intention or decision to move across the room, start a chain of neuronal firing pattern, causing the action of my crossing the room. This is a decision made out of the free will.

Are these free decisions really free? Do they not have a cause? Why we have taken one decision and not the other? If the decision is a result of certain happenings in the past? If the decision-making is out of some random process? What would cause the agent to act in a particular manner?

Probably thinking in like manner, we may say the actions are caused rather than entirely free and my decision to move across the room was not entirely free. Nevertheless, we just have a pretty strong subjective feeling that we are free. Why should we disbelieve our subjective experiential feeling? If we feel that we have free will, we should seriously consider that we have free will.

The determinism that we have no free will directly follow from reductionism. In reductionism, our mind or mental states are reduced to its substrate brain states, which are states of physical matter. And the physical world is deterministic. Wherefrom free will can come?

Determinists argue that we still feel that we have free will because our actions depend on all sorts of external and internal invisible causes that happen in our unconscious and subconscious brains.

Dualism conceives that mind stuff and brain stuff are different and the mind and body interact and affect each other. Here the mind can act as a causal agency to make us feel of free will.

Nature vs. nurture

In biology also, the question related to free will can be addressed by nature versus nurture debate. Nature refers to the genetic and hereditary factors that influence our physical appearance to personality characteristics. Nurture refers to the environment and external variables like our experiences, our upbringing, our social relations that may influence the way we talk, behave and respond to the things around us.

It is found that fraternal twins, who are twins developed from two separate embryos, raised apart have remarkable similarities in many respects, yet the environment of their own places causes several differences in the way they behave.

Identical twins develop from a single fertilized egg, so they have the same genetic material to start with. Therefore, the differences in their personality traits are due to their environment.

For example, for twins with Alzheimer, 50% of identical twins share the disease. It means there is a strong genetic component in susceptibility to Alzheimer disease. However, the fact that both identical twins do not develop the disease 100% of the time indicates that other factors like environmental variables are also involved.

Neuroscience of free will

In 1983 Benjamin Libet at the University of California, San Francisco, set up an experiment to find out the role of consciousness and free will in the voluntary act through the physiological facts of the voluntary act.

He did an experiment in which volunteers were asked to choose a random moment to flick their wrist while he used the EEG (electroencephalography) to record the brain activity of the volunteers. The volunteers were asked to report the moment on the timer clock when they had felt the conscious urge to move.

Libet found that there was a 200 ms delay, on an average, between the urge and the movement itself. However, he also found that there was a build-up of the brain potential, on an average, 550 ms before the reported conscious urge to flick the wrist. This is called the readiness potential (RP) which is present in the brain before the conscious will for action.

Libet's experimental findings suggest that subconscious neural processes determine our actions before we are ever aware of making a decision.

Since then, this experiment is quoted as evidence that free will is an illusion because the brain prepares to act well before the conscious moment to move as if a sign of the brain planning and preparing to move.

It is a blow to think that voluntary acts are initiated by a conscious decision to act. It seems contradictory to the belief that free will determines our voluntary acts.

In 2009, Judy Trevena and Jeff Miller of the University of Otago, New Zealand, did an experiment to relook at readiness potential. They also used EEG but instead of letting their volunteers decide when to move, they asked them to wait for an audio tone. After hearing the tone, volunteers were to decide if to tap the key or not.

If Libet's interpretation of readiness potential representing a decision to move was correct, then, they reasoned that readiness potential (RP) should be greater after the tone when a person chose to tap the key.

However, they found while there was an RP before volunteers made their decisions to move, the signal was the same whether or not they tapped the key.

The researchers concluded that the RP might just be a sign that the brain was paying attention and did not indicate that the brain was preparing to move.

In their second experiment, Miller and Trevena also failed to find any kind of evidence of subconscious decision-making.

Here also, the volunteers were to tap the key after hearing the tone. After the tone, they were to decide whether to tap the key with their left hand or right hand.

As movements in the right hand will depend upon the brain signals in the left hemisphere and left-hand movement will be correlated to the brain signals of the right hemisphere, they reasoned that if the unconscious processes were driving these decisions of choosing hands it should be reflected in the brain recordings.

However, they found no correlation between the signals and the chosen hand.

However, what the readiness potential meant was still not clear from their experiments.

In 2012, Aaron Schurger and his team from France gave an explanation for readiness potential build-up. They reasoned that there happen random fluctuations of neural activity in the brain. And the movement is triggered when this neural noise accumulates and crosses a threshold.

They simulated such a neural accumulator on the computer model. In this simulation, each time the neural noise build-up crossed the threshold level it marked a decision to move. In this model, the pattern of neural noise build-up reaching the threshold level and making a decision to move looked like a readiness potential.

The team devised the Libet's experiment but here the volunteers while waiting to act spontaneously were to act immediately after hearing a click. They reasoned that the fastest response to the click would be seen in those in whom the accumulation of neural noise would be most near to the threshold. This neural noise accumulation was to show up in EEG as a readiness potential.

This is exactly what the team found. The volunteers with slower responses to click were those in whom the readiness potential was well below the threshold level in the EEG recordings.

While Libet had argued that RP indicated that our brain has already decided to move well before we have a conscious intention to move, Schurger found that readiness potential is not the brain's pre-conscious process of a conscious decision to move rather it does not reflect a decision at all. Readiness potential is appearing because of neural noise build up as the nature of spontaneous brain activity.

Based on this experiment Schurger says about free will, "if we are correct then the Libet experiment does not count as evidence against the possibility of conscious will."

Anil Seth, a neuroscientist at the University of Sussex, UK opines that in Libet's experiment when the volunteers said they felt an urge to act, that urge is an experience of volition, similar to an experience of smell or taste.

American Philosopher Alfred Mele has argued that claims that scientists have concluded that free will is an illusion are not reasonable. He explains that even if the movement may have been initiated before one becomes consciously aware of it, one's conscious self can still approve, modify, or perhaps cancel the action.

These studies are providing us with good insights in understanding the neural basis of the conscious experience of volition.

The question, if a voluntary act is initiated by a conscious decision to act and the physiological signatures of the voluntary act give us a probe to look into the neuroscience of free will. Probing deep into free will is important, as the experience of having free will is the everyday experience of our consciousness.

Definition of free will by Keith Farnsworth

We perform an act of moving our arm to pick the piece of bread almost infallibly. How the neuron firings could have brought it about.

Keith Douglas Farnsworth, a researcher from the UK writes that plants seem to follow the light, bacteria move along the chemical gradient, cells perform collective actions as in organs of multicellular organism and animals appear to perform goal-directed behaviours. These seemingly goal-directed behaviours indicate that the cause of these actions, at least in part, is being generated from within the organism and is not being determined only by the chain of cause and effect relations as described by laws of physics. This seeming causal autonomy in the behaviour of an organism cannot be entirely accounted for by saying that such behaviours might have come about through evolution.

In the physicalistic world of matter, forces, and chemistry, spontaneity at most can arise from random events that may happen, at best, due to thermal noise or quantum fluctuations at microscopic levels.

Goal-directed behaviours in living systems are hardly random. They are definitely organised and can be said to be caused by a biological agency, which demands scientific explanation. According to Walker and Davies, the information has played a vital role not only in the transition to life from matter but also in the actions of day-to-day life. How biological agency, if totally material, can appear to obey the control of information even though the information has no momentum, force or energy.

Thus, the most significant feature of the life of being an autonomous agency seems incompatible with the materialistic conceptions of life. Even unicellular organisms like paramecium exhibit the essential autonomous behaviours. How the standard laws of physics can account for such autonomous behaviour? Does it indicate the requirement of some new law?

Farnsworth, in his article 'can a robot have free will?' has defined the free will as the condition in which all of the following are jointly true-

"FW1- there exists a definite entity to which agency may (or may not) be attributed;

FW2- there are viable alternative actions for the entity to select from;

FW3- it is not constrained in the exercising of two or more of the alternatives;

FW4- its will is generated by non-random process internal to it;

FW5- in similar circumstances it may act otherwise according to a different internally generated will;"

The free will researcher Farnsworth who view agency of free will in the information patterns considers that information is embodied in the arrangement of the biomolecular components relative to one another and the possible interactions among them. Identity and cause of the behaviour of an organism are due to the information pattern embodied and not due to the material embodying that information.

Free will attributable only to a conscious mind

We need to identify the entity exercising free will. We live in a world in which the idea of free will is inseparable from moral responsibilities which assumes that moral responsibility for one's actions can only be attributed to a conscious human mind.

Free will is attributable only to a conscious mind. It will be difficult to attribute it to a zombie body or to a neural structure. An algorithm incorporating a model of self and decision rules certainly cannot be said to have a moral responsibility for its actions so robots cannot be attributed any free will.

If we associate free will with the conscious mind then we would have to locate it in the wetware of our brains. There is an idea that consciousness is not located in a particular part or process of the brain but rather is emergent from the integrated whole. Then, how free will can be generating from this spread of consciousness? Therefore, the search and explanation of free will are closely tied with the search and explanation of consciousness.

Chapter 6

What maintains the continuity of personal identity?

The experience of being a person is the most familiar experience to all of us and we take it for granted. However, philosophically, the matter of personal identity wants us to consider the logically necessary and sufficient conditions for sameness of the person across time. We want to consider the conditions under which a person at one time is the same person at another time. How does his personal identity persist through time? What are those things that preserve personal identity through time?

Body identity theory

The most natural thing that a person is the same since birth until death is body continuity.

The gradual changes are happening in the body, as the person grows and ages yet his identity is recognisable because of the sameness of his body.

Although, almost all the cells of his body have been replaced anew except the brain neuronal cells yet this replacement builds up the new matter and gets rid of old matter gradually so that continuous existence of the fully functional body is maintained.

Organs may be transplanted. Like the thought experiment of Ship of Theseus, the components of the ship are replaced as the old parts began to rot. Yet identity as the old ship is maintained, as the design and function remain the same.

What happens in case the whole head is transplanted? In such a case, we may not be sure. Therefore, body identity cannot be said to be a sufficient criterion for personal identity.

Memory Theory of personal identity

A thought experiment is suggested to infer the idea where the personal identity of a person resides.

Suppose there are two persons, person A and person B. Now a mad scientist transfers the memories, behaviour, and personality of person A to person B and Person B to Person A body. He asks to choose who should get a reward of millions in cash and who should get the punishment of flogging. Will the person choose as per his body identity or as per his identity of memory-character?

John Locke considered that personal identity resides in having consciousness (memory) continuity. He believed that the person retains experiential memories of himself at different points of his life and this chain of memories makes one the same person over time.

We do not remember every moment of our lives. Like we may not remember what we ate in dinner last week, yet we seem to remember the experiential memories that link us to be the same person as us.

However, memory identity theory has its own lapses. We do not seem to remember our first two, three years of childhood.

In old age, our memories fade away. One may develop dementia. Even then we may be the same person but with a problem.

Soul identity theory

In case of dualistic concepts of the mind-body relationship, mental states associated with the brain states are said to reside in an immaterial soul that transcends the physical body. Then, one is tempted to identify the personal identity with his soul identity, as this immaterial soul would be persisting despite the changes in the body substance.

However, in cases of reincarnation, we tend to say that they have the same soul but different personal identity.

Mind transfer, a futuristic scenario

The futuristic scenario claims that transfer of your mind to the computer or a robot will be possible. One can attain immortality through such human-computer mind transfer. Body appearance and body ability would be quite different but Ray Kurzweil and American physicist Michio Kaku believe that fundamental identity can be transferred.

Question of personal identity may be important from an individualistic point of view. From a societal point of view, the value of any person may be thought in terms of his ever spoken words, his ever written words, what he has ever seen, heard, read, or visualised, what he has ever thought or attempted to think, his actions, behaviours, creations or contributions. Now, even in the present scenario, rather than a futuristic scenario, all these activities of the person can be digitally recorded and stored on a computer. The whole of a person since birth until death, every moment of it can be stored digitally. Moreover, the value of the person for society is the cost of storage of such data of a person's life. Even more, much of it can be utterly valueless and so the actual valuable storage space can be even lesser and his value to the society can be a simple hard disk.

So the personal identity is not only transferrable from mind to computer in a futuristic scenario but his personal identity manifested through spoken or written words, read, heard, seen or visualised things, his inner thoughts, his actions, creations, and contributions can be transferred to the digital storage even in the present scenario.

In my view, such a transfer of one's identity to the computer does not make the computer conscious.

Chapter 7

The altered states of Consciousness -Sleep state, Hypnosis, Anaesthesia, Hallucinations, Lucid dreams, Meditation

Sleep state

The normal state of consciousness can be said to be a state of alert and awake. Sleep is a periodic, natural, reversible state of consciousness where the person loses his sensory consciousness during his sleep time.

In our lives, time is a very valuable thing. However, we spend about 8 hrs daily in sleep. We may ask if sleep is a waste of time or sleep is the royal road to unconscious.

Sleep is physiologically necessary. In an experiment in 1983, Allan Rechtschaffen and colleagues showed that rats totally deprived of sleep suffered severe health consequences and they ultimately died.

We also experience that lack of sleep deteriorates our physical health, mental health, and mood.

During sleep, body temperature, heart rate, and brain oxygen consumption decrease. The brain especially requires sleep for repair and removing waste, which builds up during the daytime. Sleep state is mediated by the melatonin hormone, which is secreted by the pineal gland in the brain. Growth hormones are also released by pituitary gland preferentially during sleep. Therefore, sleep supports growth also, which is why babies sleep for a lot of time. Sleep is useful for mental functions and memory consolidation is supposed to occur during sleep time.

During sleep, we lose the sensory perceptions and motor functions, two important criteria of our consciousness. However, if we put the EEG (Electroencephalogram) machine then we can see a lot of brain activity underneath this loss of consciousness.

Sleep stages defined in EEG patterns

Sleep is comprised of two states; one, which is called rapid eye movement (REM) sleep, and the other, is non-rapid eye movement (NREM) sleep. Brain waves start to slow a little bit and you go through a series of stages, which are defined by EEG patterns.

NREM sleep has stage1, stage 2 and stage 3 and you can tell the stage that the person is in, based on the EEG pattern. After going through the three stages of non-REM sleep, you pop into REM sleep. Therefore, during sleep, the person goes through 90-110 minutes cycles of NREM and REM sleep. Each stage has its characteristic signature, like, stage 2 has spindles that look like oscillations of 9 to 15 cycles per second, stage 3 has slow waves of 1 to 2 cycles per second, and from there you go into REM sleep.

EEG under REM sleep is very active. In REM sleep you have rapid eye movement but has decreased muscle tone so that you have sort of sleep paralysis. Most of your dreaming occurs during REM sleep and physiologically, your breathing and heart rate might be a little bit more irregular. In contrast, in NREM sleep, you have more muscles tone, more regular heart rate, and breathing pattern. You sleepwalk during non-REM sleep. You do not sleepwalk during REM sleep. During REM sleep, you have an active brain but relaxed or paralyzed body; during non-REM sleep, you have sort of inactive brain but preserved muscle tone.

Clinicians and researchers have successfully used these different stages of sleep defined by EEG patterns to relate sleep physiology to functional neuroanatomy, consolidation of memory and sleep disorders.

Sleep medication generally reduces your arousal level and perhaps reducing anxiety and hoping that your natural sleeping mechanisms will take over.

Dreams and their significance

During the REM stage of sleep, the brain gets vivid dreams. During dreams, your sensory apparatus is disconnected, yet you have the experiences of apparent sensations of all types especially vision and movement. Dreams may also contain sounds including speech and conversation as well as felt states of pleasure, fear, and pain. Dreams may have a storyline filled with actors and scenarios and hallucinatory images.

Sigmund Freud considered that dreams could be seen as a fulfilment of a repressed wish of the subconscious mind. However, nowadays, it is said that dreams are caused by the random firing of neurons in the sensory cortex activated by brainstem (e.g. PGO waves) while forebrain tries to make a story to make some meaning out of this neuronal firing. They do not contain any hidden meaning or significance.

Thus, in dreams, our brains generate by itself an entire world of conscious experiences while being disconnected from the environment. How does the brain realize this remarkable feat? What do dreams reflect on the organisation and activity of the brain?

Hypnosis

Hypnosis is different from either sleep or waking condition in several respects.

It is a non-ordinary state, in which the mind is aware but is not in its complete wakeful condition. Hypnosis is a unique form of conscious awareness in which verbal suggestions of a hypnotist are capable of eliciting pronounced changes in subject's perception and behaviour. Here, clearly, mental representations override the physiology of the brain.

In hypnosis, the person has a narrowed focus of attention and increased responsiveness to suggestions. The hypnotist induces the person into a trance-like state by suggesting to him that he feels relaxed and sleep. During hypnosis, the person appears to take suggestions from the hypnotist only and typically responds in an involuntary fashion while ignoring the environment around him.

Trance is a mental state of response in which the person does not seem to have conscious control over his actions or thoughts but in which they can see and hear things.

The concept of hypnotic trance seems to have started with the stage shows of German physician Franz Mesmer (1770) who used to induce trance-like state on the subjects for healing purposes. He then called it animal magnetism or fluidism, as he, then, said that an invisible substance, a kind of fluid flows between the subject and therapist who is a hypnotist or the magnetizer. Although he used this mesmerisation for healing purposes only, an enquiry by Franklin held his animal magnetism claims as a sham. No such fluid flow or energy transfer or magnetic effects took place. However, the interest in its therapeutic potential persisted in the medical sphere. Under hypnosis, the person can show suggested alterations in physiology, stimuli, sensations, emotions, thoughts or behaviours and even memory.

Hypnosis is an altered state of consciousness

Brain imaging studies confirm that hypnosis is an altered state of consciousness.

A study by Stanford University researchers (2016) identified brain areas altered during hypnotic trances. They found that highly suggestible people had

i) A decrease in activity in the dorsal anterior cingulate, which is a part of the brain's salience network involved in the emotional evaluation of errors and worrying. Under hypnosis, one remains so deeply absorbed that he does not worry about anything else.

ii) Increased connectivity between dorsolateral prefrontal cortex and insula, which may be responsible for brain processing and controlling what is going on in the body.

iii) Reduced connectivity between the dorsolateral prefrontal cortex and default mode network including posterior cingulate cortex, which represents a disconnect between actions and the awareness of the actions.

Induction process generally includes asking the person to focus attention on an object so that the person gets entirely absorbed with one idea or a train of ideas while getting indifferent to every other object, purpose, or action.

Hypnosis shows the influence of the mind upon the body. Hypnosis suggestion has been used as a technique to study the basic science question of human consciousness. It is also a method of psychotherapy for a broad range of symptoms. A hypnotic trance state is not therapeutic by itself. Nevertheless, specific suggestions put to subjects in a trance state can significantly alter their behaviour even after they are brought out of their trance state. Hypnosis has been used effectively in treatments for stress, anxiety and in the treatment the phobias and chronic pain.

Anaesthesia

Anaesthesia is used in medical and surgical procedures. It means 'loss of sensation'. In the procedure, a drug or combination of drugs is used to induce reversible loss of consciousness so that invasive procedures and surgeries can be operated upon the patient.

Local anaesthesia and general anaesthesia are the two common types of medical procedures. Local anaesthesia is often used during minor procedures where a small area of the body is numbed but the patient remains fully conscious. Lidocaine is the local anaesthetic. Local anaesthetic blocks the local nerves from sending the signals to the brain, so the person, even under the invasive procedure, does not feel pain.

General anaesthesia is generally used for major operations. General anaesthesia induces unconsciousness in the patient and it prevents pain sensations and also causes muscles to be completely relaxed so that he is not able to move his limbs during operation. General anaesthesia works by acting on the central nervous system, which includes the brain and spinal cord. A person does not remember anything during the period of anaesthesia, as he is not able to form memories.

In western medicine, diethyl ether was the first common anaesthetic. Nitrous oxide was also the anaesthetic agent. However, nowadays ether derivatives like sevoflurane are more common.

Harnessing anaesthesia and brain imaging for the study of human consciousness

There exists a subjective inner experience of felt states of colour, heat, and pain. This subjective inner feeling of experience is called the hard problem of consciousness. How can subjective experiences of sensations, thoughts, and feelings arise out of physical brain matter and its physical activities?

Many philosophers think this hard problem in terms of mind-body duality. However, interaction problem remains as to how the mental subjective world of consciousness interacts with the physical sensory and motor mechanisms of the brain and the body.

Many hardcore physicalists think there is not any need to think beyond the brain and body. They do not accept that there can be any different stuff of soul but still consider that consciousness, the inner subjective feelings of the person, needs explanation and it may be an emergent property of the brain neuronal interconnections.

We feel the seamless integration and interaction of the mental states and physical brain and body in our everyday lives yet no scientific theory has been able to explain as to how the non-material subjective phenomenon of consciousness can arise out of the physical matter of brain and body. Even the scientific community more or less accepts that consciousness is a hard problem to deal with and is still a challenge for modern science.

Anaesthesia offers a safe way to modulate the status of consciousness in a reversible manner and therefore can be a useful technique of research for consciousness.

With advances in neuroimaging techniques like functional magnetic resonance imaging (fMRI), it is possible to pinpoint the brain structures or say neural mechanisms responsible for changes in consciousness. What, why, and how of the emergence of the consciousness may be found out by studying the consciousness with the help of such tools.

When we are anaesthetized, we become unconscious and our reflexes, sensations, memory vanishes. Anaesthetics seem to induce unconsciousness by blocking the brain's ability to integrate information. The cellular and modular mechanisms of anaesthetic are not completely understood but are thought to work by blocking the ion channels that regulate synaptic transmission in the neuronal membranes in key regions of the brain and spinal cord.

Although sleep and anaesthesia are different things yet neurotransmitters, neural circuitry and electrical patterns in both these altered states of consciousness show significant overlap. This suggests that anaesthetics may be achieving their loss of consciousness by acting through the same normal sleep and arousal systems of the brain.

Few persons have reported to have dreams or have reported the consciousness of the procedure despite having no indication of it under anaesthesia unconsciousness and its monitoring. During anaesthesia, if a person dreams it can be said that it is an intriguing aspect of subjective conscious experience.

However, some researchers believe that people may retrieve bits of conversations and remember dreams during the wearing out phase of anaesthesia called the emergence or maybe that the person has not been made fully unconscious due to lack of dosage.

When performing general anaesthesia, state of unconsciousness is induced under reliable, controllable, and reversible conditions. How anaesthesia works and how it affects the different brain and body parts may be an important method of scientific research regarding consciousness.

It is increasingly evident from many studies involving different anaesthetics and multiple neuroimaging techniques that unconsciousness induced by anaesthetics is characterized by a functional fragmentation of cortical and thalamocortical connections.

This reversible fragmentation is broadly supportive of the integrated information theory of consciousness (Tononi 2004) and other perspectives of the neurobiology on conscious experiences.

EEG recordings from the scalp reflect the changes in neuronal firing pattern as anaesthesia is given to the patient. These change from the low-voltage, high-frequency pattern of wakefulness (beta waves pattern) to the slow-wave EEG of deep sleep and then to an EEG of the unconscious brain.

If we monitor the brain activity through EEG, we can see that the brain is not turned off during anaesthesia rather we see specific patterns in EEG.

Different general anaesthetics like propofol, ketamine, sevoflurane, dexmedetomidine have different EEG signatures. Dexmedetomidine produces the EEG pattern similar to NREM sleep.

In our studies, we find that so many differently structured anaesthetics, which bind to different receptors in the brain and their mechanisms different, can produce the same endpoint result-loss of consciousness. Like, propofol affects the GABA neurotransmitters. When GABA receptors are activated, ions channels in the neuronal membrane open up and cause the ions to flow in the neuron, effectively, causing the firing in a nerve cell to shut off.

Propofol is generally given intravenously. When it enters the brain, it travels through a major blood vessel passing through the brainstem and there it interacts with GABA receptors and turns off arousal centres.

Therefore, anaesthetic makes effective changes in the inhibitory functions of the neurons and then its result is that signalling between different areas of the brain is disrupted. They are not able to interact with each other now. Therefore, if communication between different parts, modules of the brain is necessary for consciousness, you lose it.

If our brain is basically a device that when fully conscious seems to calculate more information, seems to be more functionally connected, seems to be less synchronous, what does that actually mean about the underlying biological stuff that produced all that?

Do brains produce consciousness simply because they are sufficiently connected and complex? Is that all we are? Can we build a machine that could be sufficiently complex that will become conscious? If we someday connect our brains to machines or to other brains, will that result in higher consciousness since it involves more connectivity?

Drugs induced altered state of consciousness

Psychoactive drugs are basically chemical substances that alter one's mood and perception. These molecules alter the states of the brain by mimicking the function of neurotransmitters.

Psychoactive drugs are of three general kinds: stimulants, depressants, hallucinogens.

Depressants: - Depressants are drugs that slow down the electrical activity of the brain. There are several different types of depressants, including alcohol, barbiturates, and benzodiazepines. These drugs generally increase the activity of the GABA neurotransmitter system. GABA has a quieting effect on the brain. Therefore, these drugs have the effect of quieting the brain. Since these drugs can slow brain activity, they are useful for treating anxiety and sleep disorders. Alcohol also acts as a disinhibitor, impairing your brain's judgment areas while reducing your self-awareness and self-control and it disrupts memory formation.

Stimulants: - Stimulants are drugs that tend to increase the overall levels of activity of the central nervous system and the body. Many of these drugs increase the activity of the dopamine neurotransmitter system. Dopamine activity is often associated with reward and craving. Drugs in this category include cocaine, Methamphetamine (meth) MDMA (ecstasy), nicotine and caffeine.

If one takes these drugs then the brain's own system of producing dopamine is reduced so one requires the increasing dose to get the same feeling of euphoria and vigour. Caffeine is a common stimulant, which is naturally found in coffee, tea or chocolate. Nicotine is found in cigarette and tobacco products.

Both physical and psychological dependence are important parts of taking stimulants and depressants.

Hallucinogens: - Hallucinogens are also called psychedelic drugs and these cause significant alteration in perceptions and induce sensory images without actual sensory inputs, which means you could end up seeing, hearing, smelling or feeling things that are not real. Mescaline and psilocybin are naturally occurring hallucinogen in plants and mushrooms while others are synthetic hallucinogens like LSD (Lysergic Acid diethylamide), DMT (Dimethyltryptamine).

Psychedelic means mind revealing. It reveals mind through the strong experiences of colour, sound, smell, taste, and touch.

Expansion of mind or consciousness may include the vivid coloured geometrical shape patterns like a kaleidoscope of colours, distortion of shape and distortions in time perception, illusions of body size variations like a feeling as if you are a giant, breathing walls, and thinking is somewhat muddled. When the eyes are open, the visual alternations are overlaid onto the objects and spaces out there in the physical environment but when the eyes are closed, the visual alternations are seen on the inner screen space behind the eyelids. Some psychedelics may produce the sensations of being disconnected from the one's body and merging of the boundary between the self and surrounding environment.

Tryptamine psychedelics like DMT and psilocybin have molecular structures that resemble serotonin neurotransmitter. Therefore, they have an affinity for serotonin receptors. These serotonergic psychedelics seem to produce the psychedelic experience by binding to serotonin receptor particularly 5-HT 2A receptor as an agonist that is they activate these receptors. These serotonin receptors are distributed throughout the neocortex, have somewhat higher levels in occipital parietal areas.

However, it is not entirely understood how this introduces the richness of mental effects but it is likely that it acts by increasing the inputs from the thalamus to the cortex and thus increasing excitations in the cortex. Thalamus is basically the major relay for sensory information input to the cortex.

Certain dissociative drugs like ketamine produce sensations of being disconnected from one's body along with the perceptual alterations seen with other psychedelics.

Ketamine is an NMDA antagonist, that is, it binds to these receptors and blocks their activity. NMDA receptors are found throughout the cerebral cortex as well as subcortically.

Although the use of psychedelics, which are banned in India can easily and profoundly change our experience of consciousness, we can also and often more safely, alter our consciousness without drugs. These altered states of consciousness are sometimes the result of simple and safe activities such as sleeping, dreaming, lucid dreaming, exercising, yoga, and meditation.

Altered states of consciousness brought out by the psychedelics allow us to see our minds and ourselves with different perspectives of perception than the ordinary mind.

A research study of psychedelic drugs on the mind

In a study conducted at the University of Sussex and Imperial College, London, the researchers imaged the activities of neurons in people's brain as they reported being high after taking the psychedelic drugs LSD, ketamine, or psilocybin. In this systematic study, the participants have taken psychedelic drugs for the scientific study of the state of consciousness under the effect of psychedelic drugs. Psilocybin is the active ingredient in magic mushrooms and ketamine acts in low doses as psychedelic but in high doses, it has an anaesthetic effect.

In the study, the researchers computed the measures of neural signal diversity form the spontaneous magneto-encephalographic (MEG) signals from participant volunteers during altered states of consciousness induced by these psychedelic substances psilocybin, ketamine and LSD.

The measure of neural signal diversity from the spontaneous recording of neural signals is a robust method to determine the conscious level. The computation of diversity of brain signals provides a mathematical index of the level of consciousness. The people in the wakeful state have more diverse neural activity than in states of sleep or anaesthesia. In the study, it was found that volunteers under the influence of psychedelic drugs like psilocybin, ketamine, and LSD show increased neural signal diversity compared with when they were in a normal waking state.

This increased diversity of signals from the brain or say the increased complexity of brain activity corresponded to the volunteer participants reporting vivid experiences and a feeling of floating and finding inner peace and the feeling that self was disintegrating.

So we can say that the brain is pushed to a higher state of consciousness and, certainly, an altered state of consciousness by the use of psychedelic drugs.

Understanding the brain basis of consciousness remains one of the outstanding challenges in modern science.

When we are conscious, our conscious experiences are populated by a variety of sensory perceptions, thoughts and feelings, language, understanding of the self and the world, free will such as to decide what to do, that collectively form an integrated conscious scene.

Intuitively we can say that increased conscious level (how conscious one is) may be related to an increased range of conscious contents (what one is conscious of when one is conscious). By the psychedelic drugs, there happens the more broad experience of consciousness contents and they are experienced without the loss of consciousness.

Lucid Dream

A lucid dream is a dream during which dreamer is aware that he is dreaming. During lucid dreaming, the dreamer may be able to exert some control over the dream characters, storyline, and environment.

It seems lucid dreaming happens to only around 20 to 30 per cent of the people. However, it is difficult to say that lucid dreaming is an evolutionary advantage. A study by Voss and colleagues (2012) found that lucid dreaming might be linked to brain development as children have more lucid dreaming than adults.

Lucid dreaming is a state between dreaming and waking. Lucid dreaming happens during REM state of sleep when you dream naturally. In lucid dreaming state, one is able to influence the story of his dream. During lucid dreams, one may get pleasurable feelings of sight, motion, happiness, and even sex, but feelings of fear, sadness, and pain are also possible in a lucid dream.

Dreams generally are of random thoughts and actions and are involuntary. However, there is a state between dreaming and awakening when we are still dreaming but are aware that we are dreaming. This can be a state of lucid dreaming. If dreaming is like a movie, an involuntary thing, lucid dreaming can be said be like a video game where one can have some volitional control over the dream characters, narrative and environment.

I myself have tried lucid dreaming and have tried flying by flapping the hands. Even when you are aware during dreaming that you cannot fly or raise or float your body, yet you feel elated when it actually happens.

Researchers do recognize that lucid dreaming is a state of dreaming that differs from both wakefulness and normal dreaming on a phenomenological level. Since phenomenological aspects have their basis in the brain states so neural correlates for these states should also, be different.

Neural correlates of lucid dreaming and comparisons with phenomenological aspects

The pattern of fMRI based neural activity images shows that lucid dreaming differs from either non-lucid dreaming or waking. It is a state between dreaming and waking. During REM sleep ventromedial prefrontal cortex, amygdala and other parts of the limbic system of the brain are activated. During lucid dreaming, dorsolateral prefrontal cortex and precuneus region are activated.

Phenomenal aspects associated with dorsolateral prefrontal cortex region are meta-awareness, working memory, decision making and conscious perception. Precuneus is a brain region involved in self-referential processing that is first-person perspective and experience of agency.

In addition to brain regions activity studies by neuro-imaging, studies have also been made to find the particular pattern of frequencies and brain waves in EEG (Electroencephalogram) patterns during lucid dreaming.

Different frequencies of cortical EEG pattern are associated with different cognitive activities and levels of consciousness. Delta waves (0-4 HZ) are usually found in deep sleep, while theta waves (4-8 HZ) are associated with sleep and drowsiness. Alpha waves (8-13 HZ) are the pattern of brain waves when the person is awake with eyes closed like in meditation and often precedes sleep. Beta waves (13-30HZ) are associated with normal waking consciousness while gamma waves (above 30HZ) are associated with learning, memory and an alert awake state. The high frequencies of waking can also be found partly in REM sleep. A study done by Holzinger, LaBerge and Levitan (2006) found that not only there was, in general, more beta-1 (13-19HZ range) in lucid dreaming compared to non-lucid REM but also less frontal beta and more parietal beta. The ratio of parietal to frontal beta-1 power was higher in lucid dreaming compared to non-lucid dreaming in REM sleep.

Lucid dreaming poses challenges to the traditional theories of dreaming because these theories presuppose that dreaming is a fully unconscious process. In a lucid dream, one has a certain degree of control and awareness and gives conscious access to the contents of the dream. Contents of the dream in lucid dreaming are hardly random.

Lucid dreaming provides a natural window to peep into the inside of the expanse of consciousness. Lucid dreaming can be said to be a way to expand consciousness boundaries.

Wakeful consciousness is characterized by the awareness of the external world, our bodies, and ourselves. During dreaming, people have perceptual and emotional experiences but typically fail to recognize their own condition. Dreams have poor memory access and limited thought capabilities.

Dream consciousness and waking consciousness are different in their respective causal pathways. Dreams represent an offline internally generated simulation of the sensory experiences. We may also ask the question if dream consciousness is a purer form of consciousness which arise as being free of interaction with the external world through our sensory apparatus.

Meditation

A person lives most of his life through three states of consciousness- waking, dreaming and sleeping.

In the waking state of consciousness, we experience the world through the senses. We seek elevation and joy from these senses.

Through our senses, we seek joy and pleasure in a bid to satiate the desires and wants of the mind so that we can get more from the physical to the mental realm. We want more and more of the physical objects to satisfy our mental wants and desires. The greed of mental wants and desires would want us to have all the wealth of the world. To get the mental satiation the person engages in more and more of worldly pleasures. To satiate the mind the person wants things to happen in his way or in a certain way. It leads to many kinds of distortions in his person yet he pursues his mental satisfaction through the prism of his worldly life.

In the sleeping state, one is resting being cut off from senses. Through dreaming, he reaches his inner consciousness but remains unaware of it.

My method of meditation

In meditation you are awake, removed from the active participation from the senses, achieve the peep into the inner world like by trying to make the image of the God Mahavira on mind's screen and chant mantra to keep you engaged in the task of meditation. By sparing some time for the meditation daily, your inner world is reflected in your trying to make the image of God and through the God's image, you get the reflection of the cosmic world around you. These lead up to the contemplation of your own world around you and as well as lead to a prayer made to the majesty of God.

Meditation renews our mental energy, heals the mind and body, and helps us to develop new ways of handling daily stressors.

I, also, am an avid 'worship meditation' doer. I do the meditation by standing before the idol of God Mahavira. When you close the eyes after seeing the idol, an afterimage of God is made on your mind's phenomenal screen. Then my attempt remains to retain the image of God and keep on making the image of God, in mind's screen while I chant my prayer, *'Bhagwan Mahavir aapki sada hi Jai ho'.* (May the people always be there to worship God Mahavira, or in other words, may the kindness of God Mahavira always remain there to bless us). Your mind may wander to all sorts of thoughts of your world. But you remain focussed on God's image or making God's image; your inner thoughts and the thoughts of your world or thoughts of the world around you interact with God's image and God's image-making process and helps you to attain more calm and bliss and helps you in dealing your daily stressors in a better way.

Sometimes meditating on God's image can be strenuous and sometimes it may give you greater mental satisfaction. In times of lean period when meditation feels strenuous, you may not overexert yourself but open the eyes, see the idol of the God and again an afterimage forms in the mind's eye. Then you meditate on the retaining of this afterimage while making your prayer to God. Many times, it becomes easier to make the image of God idol you have seen in the temple. You can easily meditate with this idol.

This will lead to increased mental satiation with the meditation and your requirement of seeking mental satiation from your physical world around you will be lessened.

Studies done on Buddhist monks show that meditation brings changes in mind

There is a study conducted by Richard Davidson of the University of Wisconsin-Madison on Buddhist monks by hooking them up for EEG testing and brain scanning. Buddhist monks had 10-15 yrs of meditation experience with them. They were asked to meditate on compassion, a feeling of love and kindness to all. It was found that Gamma ~40 HZ activity in the brain happened with much larger amplitudes than the controls who were non-experienced meditators and the oscillations across all frequencies from various parts of the cortex were more synchronized.

Buddhist monks told that during their meditation they tried to generate a mental state in which thoughts of compassion permeates the whole mind with no other thoughts.

Gamma waves are thought to be an indication of coordination and integration of far-flung brain circuits and are an indication of the state of a higher state of consciousness than normal awake state consciousness.

Using the brain scan called functional magnetic resonance imaging the researchers tried to find the regions that were active during compassion meditation. It was found that monk's brains had enhanced activity in the left prefrontal cortex as compared to controls. The left prefrontal cortex is the site associated with thoughts and emotions such as happiness while the right prefrontal cortex is the site of negative emotions and anxiety. Such things were never seen before from purely mental activity.

The mental practice through the meditation of Buddhist monks had an effect on their brain in the same way as tennis practice enhances performance.

Davidson found that meditation not only changes the workings of the brain at the time of meditation only but also, quite possibly, produces permanent changes. This finding was based on the fact that monks had enhanced gamma activity than the control group even before they started meditating.

These kinds of brain researches provide objective evidence that mental discipline and meditative practice can change the workings of the brain.

In one of the study, researchers from National University of Singapore studied the claims of Tibetan Buddhists who practice g-tummo meditation that they can dry the wet clothes wrapped around their naked bodies in minus cold temperatures of Himalayas by meditation. Therefore, a study was conducted to measure the core body temperature increase during simply the breathing and during breathing and visualizing. In g-tummo meditation breathing technique is called vase breathing where after inhaling the breath they hold it for some time and then contract the abdominal pelvic muscles to exhale the air.

Visualization is done by visualizing a flame rising to the head along with each breath. The study found that meditators were able to increase their core body temperatures to 38.3 degrees. They found that high core temperature was achieved when forceful breathing was combined with visualization whereas during forceful breathing alone temperature was increased but remained in the range of normal body temperature.

The study also showed that even non-mediators who performed that technique of breathing and mental imaging could increase their core body temperature to some extent.

This makes us think that thoughts and mental disciplines can affect the brain's neural states while the use of drugs shows that the brain's neural state changes construct a different mental reality for us. Thoughts and pattern of thoughts are immaterial stuff which affects the material stuff of the brains neuronal circuitry.

Chapter 8

Near-death experience, Reincarnation, Terminal lucidity

Near-Death Experience

Can consciousness function independent of the brain or is it the construct of the brain itself in some emergent manner? Near-death experiences that some people report who return to life after being at the threshold of death may give us some thoughts to ponder over if consciousness can be thought of as an independent entity delinked from the brain.

A near-death experience, a person experiences at the threshold of death where he could have died but returned to life by a quirk of fate, has many features. The person reaches clinical death, his heart stopped pumping, his breath has failed, and his brain activity mapped through EEG also shows flat, yet in such situations, the person is resuscitated and revived. During such periods, the person has the experiences where he feels that he was detached from his body and passed through the dark tunnel, saw the bright light and met angels and God, met his deceased relatives. He often describes a feeling of peace and calmness and painlessness, life review as life events flash before his view, somebody asking him to go back to life, which is often accompanied by his resistance to return, feeling as if returned back to his body.

People from all over the world report near-death experiences and their narratives sometimes correspond to their cultural and religious beliefs.

There seems to be no correspondence between the vivid and detailed narrative of near-death experiences and his brain and body physiology at the time of such experience.

A study by Sam Parnia in NDEs

A large study AWARE (AWAreness during REsuscitation) in near-death experiences, spread over four years, was conducted by Dr Sam Parnia and team. The University of Southampton, UK sponsored the study and the results of the study were published in the year 2014. This was a four-year international study on 2060 cardiac arrest events out of which 140 were cardiac arrest survivors from 15 hospitals in the United Kingdom, the United States, and Austria. 101 survivors completed the questionnaire.

The study found that thirty-nine per cent of survivors described a perception of awareness but did not have explicit recall of events. This suggests that more people may have mental activity but forgets their memories after recovery either due to the drugs used during reviving procedure or due to the effects of brain injury.

Only 9 per cent had reported experiences which could be categorised as NDE and 2 per cent reported OBE (out of body experience) having recalled of seeing and hearing events during anaesthesia. One had a verifiable period of conscious awareness of auditory stimuli during which time the cerebral function was not expected.

The study concluded that recalled experiences in relation to death and subsequent revival, at least, merit further genuine investigation without prejudice.

Study of NDEs in blind persons

Dr Kenneth Ring and Sharan Cooper (1999) studied the NDEs of blind people. They narrate the NDE experience of Vicki Umipeg, a forty-five-year-old blind woman. This blind woman was born blind as her optic nerve got completely destroyed at birth in the incubator itself because of an excess of oxygen. Her NDE experience was feature-rich where she saw and heard and met people and she had an out of body experience; she also saw trees and flowers, saw her dead friends and grandmother, tunnel and light, during her NDE.

A study by Von Lommel in NDEs

Van Lommel and team 2001 in their study in near-death experiences in the Netherlands found that near-death experiences do not have a physical or medical root. A purely physiological explanation such as cerebral anoxia for NDEs does not explain why only 18 per cent of patients had NDE and not 100 per cent.

They discuss that NDE pushes at the limits of medical ideas about the range of human consciousness and the mind-brain relation. The patients who were clinically dead (flat EEG, showing no electrical activity in the cortex and loss of brain stem function evidenced by fixed dilated pupils and absence of gag reflex) but were resuscitated back, have reported feature-rich NDEs. They concluded that if really the consciousness and memories are localized in the brain, should be discussed and the theory and background of transcendence should be included as a part of an explanatory framework for these experiences.

Possible explanations for NDE

NDE represent evidence that an immaterial soul or mind exists which would leave the body upon death.

Irreducible mind proposes that the mind is not created by the brain and the mind can work independently from the brain reviving the concept of dualism. Charles Bruce Greyson, an NDE researcher from the University of Virginia, argues for dualism but scientific studies do not accept this view.

Many scientists refute the afterlife claims of NDE researchers. Their opinions are based on beliefs in materialism and they argue of lack of data in NDE research to substantiate their belief. Science tells that life is physics and chemistry and biology is based completely on the arrangement of matter and molecules and their chemistry. Our ability to have meaning and to have subjective experiences is really a by-product or side effect of the evolution of matter, which is mostly driven by random processes.

NDE at best still requires a satisfactory explanation.

NDEs may be a kind of predetermined response construct as if a psychological defence mechanism in mind itself in response to the stress of our encounter with death. It may be getting triggered by the underlying stressed brain state of NDE times.

It is also suggested that NDEs may be a form of reliving the trauma of birth through the birth canal. The dying brain may have been recreating the passage through a tunnel to light, warmth, and affection. However, NDEs happen to those persons also who were born through C-section.

Many materialists argue with the 'dying brain hypothesis' for NDEs put forward by psychology professor Susan Blackmore. She says that NDE is merely the result of hallucinations from the brain that happens as the brain malfunctions and collapses as a result of low oxygen levels and is, in fact, an artefact of brain structures and brain chemistry. According to the dying brain hypothesis, there is no soul within the body. Body and brain are totally material in nature and so the explanation for NDE is to be found in materialistic philosophy only.

Alex Petrov, associate professor at Ohio State University, says that there can be two main arguments in claiming that NDEs are the construct of dying brain only.

NDEs are similar around the world and throughout history. The consistency in NDEs may be because everyone has the same set of brain hormones and neuronal systems and same brain functioning. That is why they have similar experiences when those systems fail.

The second argument maintains that all the features of NDE can occur under other conditions also, not near death, and therefore NDEs should be explained in terms of hallucinations or normal imagery happening due to brain.

Susan Blackmore's dying brain hypothesis says that-

Oxygen deficiency can cause the occurrences of seeing tunnels, seeing a light and hearing music.

An excessive release of endorphins at the time of death may cause euphoria associated with a near-death episode.

The actions of endorphins and neurotransmitters may cause such cerebral structures as the hippocampus, which is associated with memory, to release stored memories resulting in life review.

Thus she, in a nutshell, provides a materialistic interpretation of near-death experience.

But as it appears that brain states that might be causing the NDE is missing. To me, it seems independent of the brain states. At most, brain state associated with NDE may be triggering the onset of the near-death experience. We cannot and should not ignore the data, which has been collected during the scientific studies into the near-death experiences, just to harp upon the reductionist materialistic explanation of near-death experiences.

In explaining near-death experience, we are not looking for the mechanistic explanation of near-death experience only but we also need to have a satisfactory explanation for the subjective experience of seeing, meeting people, hearing voices, memories formation in near-death experiences. As Kevin Williams says that, we should not seek only the television components (brain structures) but should also seek an explanation for the television show (the subjective experiences).

Can near-death experiences be a construct of the brain while the EEG shows nil brain activity? So at least it should be understood that to have subjective experiences, the brain's neural correlates are not a must condition.

In the case of NDE experiences, as shown by Sam Parnia, brain activity pattern become flatlined but the brain cells themselves do not cease their activity, they do not become dead.

Sam Parnia has suggested that a possible way to explain NDE can be that mind is mediated by the brain, but is not produced by the brain.

However, Susan Blackmore finds purely physical explanations to be more reasonable. She agrees up to this point only that NDEs are just the recollections of what happens, as consciousness is lost or as it is regained, but not while in unconsciousness.

Since materialists assume that, there is no soul in the body, then mind and its characteristics like the experiences of seeing, hearing, memory, understanding, free will all must be the construct of the materialistic body and the brain somehow. It might be the pattern of neural connections or the sum of the parts is more than the parts itself.

However, when we attribute physical laws to matter then they get assigned to its smallest of its constituents like the electric field to the charge and magnetic field to the moving charge, gravitational force to the mass of the particle. Sometimes the argument is given that bulk of water molecules has the property of fluidity, viscosity, wetting etc. but individual molecules of water cannot be said to have these properties. Therefore, the bulk of the neurons and their interconnections may somehow create the property of mind. Some features of NDE experience singly or in multiple features can happen when the brain is not totally dysfunctional, I may not be in denial of that but the fact that in NDE underlying brain activity seems to have come to a stop, it gives an extreme perspective and evidence to ponder to consider the mind-body problem in dualistic terms.

In the face of evidence from near-death experiences and studies, that brain activity is flat during NDE leaves no alternative but to delink the mind and brain. It gives us a question to think if the brain is necessary for the mind. The near-death experience evidence tells us that the brain may not be a precondition for the mind experiences.

I am of the view that we should not outrightly reject the evidence or experiences stated by near-death experiencers as a figment of the imagination. Materialist comes to close of explaining NDE as dying brain phenomenon and dying brain construct somehow. However, this comes to contradiction when we come to know that the brain shows the nil activity in EEG graphs which, at least, show that the brain is at an undetectable level of activity at best.

If the brain were responsible for thinking and construction of the mind reality, then, when it is dying one would expect this thinking and construct to be disordered or less clear. However, clarity expressed in narratives of near-death experiences is an argument to build for the thought of mind-body duality. It is the soul in somewhat a free state due to which the person has clarity in experience and retention of this NDE.

Drugs seem to affect the brain physiology and in a way affect the soul's connection to the body and experiences of hallucinations or out of the body etc. produced by the drugs is the soul's response in terms of the new reality of brain states, which have been affected by the drugs.

Encounters with deceased relatives in NDEs

Bruce Greyson, a well-known NDE researcher, from the University of Virginia gives examples of encounters with deceased persons during NDE, which seriously challenges the materialistic model of consciousness and the brain. An American doctor, Dr K.M. Dale treated a nine-year-old boy for meningitis who fought near death for 36 hours. His parents were always there near him providing him care and vigil in the hospital. When he was successfully treated, he talked to his parents.

The boy described that he had gone to heaven where he saw several of his deceased relatives. He also told that he had also met his sister Teresa and Teresa told him that he had to go back to his body. This made the boy's father very upset as Teresa was at her college 1500 km away and was perfectly healthy. His father then tried to telephone Teresa at her college. He learned that the college officials were trying unsuccessfully to reach the family to tell them the tragic news that Teresa had, in fact, got killed around midnight in a vehicle accident.

This example and such other encounters the people tell of meeting deceased people during their NDEs tell that consciousness, soul or spirit may survive the death or substantiates afterlife hypothesis.

My temptation is to consider dualism as an explanation for NDEs

One is to consider as somehow being constructed by the brain and one is to consider as reflective of the true nature of the soul and its characteristics. I feel the temptation to consider that there is a soul inside our bodies somehow interacting with the brain and body.

Dualism temptation is so great. People do not like to think of themselves as just a body but do have a popular escape mechanism in the conception of soul, spirit, consciousness.

In this book, I have tried to explain the mind-body problem in terms of different stuff explanation for the mind and the body. I want to explain the mind-body problem in terms of substance dualism and how this different substance of the mind is interacting with the brain and body. This offers an explanation for NDE experiences also.

Rebirth or Reincarnation

If consciousness is produced by the brain then if the person dies his brain dies, consciousness ends; it cannot continue in other life. However, there are cases where some children seem to remember their past lives.

Bruce Greyson in his talk on YouTube 'is consciousness produced by the brain', talks about the research carried out into the subject of the reincarnation by Ian Stevenson of the University of Virginia.

Ian Stevenson has made his study into reincarnation and discovered evidence suggesting that memories and physical injuries can be transferred from the past life to present life. He investigated about 2500 cases of children from all over the world who recalled having past lives. Children from Asian countries like India, Sri Lanka, Burma, Lebanon etc. and from European countries and also from America were investigated for their unusual abilities to recall past life memories.

Mostly the recall of memories in these children happens between age two to five and those memories fade, as they grow older. In about 60% of the cases, the past life remembered ended violently either in tragic accidents or intentional wounds.

The average time that passes between the death in the past life and the birth in the present life is 12 years but happened at short interval also. It was possible that in some cases in a past life the person was a man whose life is remembered by a girl in the present life and vice versa. It was also possible that a Hindu child was remembering the past life of a Muslim person. The person of the past life many times lived at a great distance or died at a distant place than the child of the present life.

In some cases, corroborative evidence is found in terms of birthmarks and birth defect. Like, in one of the cases from India, a child Lekhpal who said he remembered the life of another person Hukam Singh who had put his right hand into the blades of a fodder-chopping machine and lost his fingers. In this birth, the child had almost absent fingers in his right hand for no reason of heredity or birth procedure.

If such cases show that, the person is reincarnated in new life. The answer is no, as, Bruce Greyson tells that the reincarnation hypothesis also does not fit into the data. Sometimes it was seen that the two children in the present life are recollecting the same past life. In addition, instances have come to the notice that the child remembering the past life was six months old when the person of past life died.

These studies find no explanation in materialism. However, in dualistic notions, these studies show that not only the soul has an afterlife but it carries the associated memories of past lives also.

Terminal lucidity

There are cases of terminal lucidity in the medical literature where the person becomes lucid and coherent in his appearance and communication despite his bad physical conditions of the brain. This usually happens just a few hours to a few days before the death time.

A typical case would be like a woman patient who has lost all ability to communicate with her visitors, with her loved ones; when they come, she does not recognize them, she does not know their names, she does not speak, and she does not seem to be even aware of her world. Then for some strong reason, just before she dies and her loved ones have come to gather around the bed, she erupts into her old personality. Her brain is all but totally destroyed but suddenly she is able to communicate with her loved ones, she speaks about her grandchildren and how they are doing, she knows everyone names, she is completely herself. This is a typical example of terminal lucidity. According to Dr Alexander Batthyany who had looked into such cases, this happens, in about 5 to 10 per cent of Alzheimer's patients.

It cannot be explained in terms of conventional brain science. These lucid moments just before death happens not because there has been a sudden correction of the physiological condition of the brain but, rather, the being, the consciousness, the soul, the person who he really is, has managed to loosen itself from the brain.

As if, it could not communicate because it was obstructed by the sick brain. These cases may be suggestive to that spirit or consciousness can operate independently of the body organ, nervous system and the brain.

Chapter 9

If the brain is necessary for consciousness

The brain is so intimately connected to the consciousness that consciousness is considered as the emergent phenomenon resulting from the interconnection and firing of the neurons. The neuroscience has plenty of evidence resulting from studies made into the functioning of the brain, like due to lesions, injuries, tumours, epilepsy etc. that brain is closely tied up with consciousness. We do not know how it is being generated from our brains but materialist view is that the brain alone is constructing consciousness for us somehow.

The feature-rich NDE happening to the people when their EEG shows flat and even the brain stem is not functioning, however, gives us a thought- maybe consciousness is somehow delinked from the brain.

Conventional and contemporary neuroscientists as a general rule all believe, in fact, they assume that the brain creates consciousness, that consciousness is a by-product or side effect of brain function and this is what is called the materialist perspective. It is the idea that reality is defined first and foremost in terms of matter that it is only material things that exist and therefore, anything else that exists, such as consciousness and subjective experience that by definition this has to be created by a material object such as the brain. And so the assumption is that anything that we think or do, not only involves our brains but requires our brain and therefore when our brain ceases to function or say when it dies, our consciousness dies too because it is dependent entirely on the brain.

Brain activity is closely connected to creating consciousness. It can be seen from the numerous correlations between brain activity and consciousness. The brain is so pervasive in maintaining the consciousness that cortical processes add even the colour and motion of objects in one's conscious experience.

Cerebral Achromatopsia is a form of loss of colour perception that is caused by damage to the area V4 of the cerebral cortex rather than abnormalities in the cells of the eye's retina and patients report seeing the world in grayscale with no colour vision. Magnetic stimulation of this same brain area V4 is correlated with chromatophenes, conscious experiences of unusual colours. If the damage to cortical area V5 happens, patients may have Cerebral Akinetopsia or motion blindness. Here the patient cannot perceive motion in their visual field; they perceive motion as a succession of stationary images.

'Is your brain really necessary?' titled article by neurologist John Lorber appeared in Science journal in

Dec 1980. It speaks that there are people in this world who have virtually no brain cortex left yet are healthy, have normal to high intelligence and normal social behaviour. John Lorber specialized in hydrocephalus cases in children.

In hydrocephalus, there is an abnormal accumulation of cerebrospinal fluid in the brain, which in turn compresses the brain tissue, which may lead to many difficulties and mental impairments and may lead to death if not treated. It is typically treated by the surgical placement of a shunt system. Lorber described many cases of children and eventually some adults who had cerebrospinal fluid filled up to 95 per cent of their skull but were apparently living normal life against all odds.

In a YouTube video, titled 'Is Consciousness Produced by the Brain?' Bruce Greyson tells the case of a young girl published in 2007. She was a high school honour student who had been accepted into college. She was injured and knocked unconscious in an accident. She had to undergo surgery. A scan of her head just before brain surgery revealed that she had no cerebral cortex at all. She had just a brain stem inside her skull. And when the surgeon opened up her skull to operate, he found exactly like that: just a brain stem and no cerebral cortex.

In a normal brain, brain stem plays an important part in the regulations of heart function, breathing, sleep cycle. Nerve connections of the motor and sensory systems of the brain to the rest of the body pass through the brain stem also and brain stem is pivotal in maintaining consciousness but cortical areas are required to perform higher-order cognitive functions like thinking, perceiving, making decisions and so on.

Hemispherectomy

Hemispherectomy is a surgical procedure, which in a rare case is performed mostly on children, down with epileptic seizures due to a broad area of one hemisphere and other treatments have not worked. Here half of the brain is removed. It is performed only on children because due to neuroplasticity, the rest of their half brain will take over of the functions of the removed half.

However, it is also performed in adults sometimes who also appear to cope well with the deficit.

Corpus Callosum severance and split-brain condition-

The corpus callosum is a thick bundle of nerve fibres connecting the left and right hemisphere of the brain. The corpus callosum communicates motor, sensory, and cognitive information between the two hemispheres.

Corpus callosum can sometimes be severed to prevent severe epilepsy. This results in a split-brain condition. This result in a lack of coordination between left and right brain and patients have little difficulty with a bimanual task like riding a bicycle. Conflicts arise sometimes between left and right brain. Suppose split-brain patients are shown an image at the left side, this will be processed by the right brain. However, speech control centres are on the left-brain. Therefore, they may not be able to speak what they have seen.

Sometimes, it can create interesting situations, like, you want to pick up a thing from the shelf with your right hand and the left hand comes and prevents it and does a sort of fight.

However, if these split-brain patients are of two minds- No; split-brain patients lead and behave a normal life. When there is a conflicting dilemma, often one hemisphere is able to override and control behaviour.

Research, done by Yair Pinto & team (2016) on split-brain patients showed that despite lack of communication between the two cerebral hemispheres there existed clear evidence for unified consciousness, i.e., one conscious agent in one brain.

Thus, arguably, can consciousness, which as popular scientific opinion is considered as a construct of the brain alone, be delinked from the brain? For consciousness to happen and exist, the brain is not the only necessary thing.

The peculiar case of planarian flatworm

Planarian flatworm has exceptional regeneration capabilities. If its brain is cut, it regenerates its brain. In an experiment, James V McConnel & Robert Thompson trained the planarian flatworms by pairing a bright light with an electric shock. After training with this pairing, they took away the electrical shock and only exposed them to bright light. The flatworms reacted to bright light as if they had been shocked. Now they cut the worm in two pieces. Each piece grew into a full-fledged planarian flatworm. It was found that both the flatworms reacted to the bright light as if they had been given an electric shock.

This shows that not only the brain may not be a necessary thing but also that memory can form without the brain.

Chapter 10

If consciousness is an emergent phenomenon

We have the stream of consciousness, an inner movie going on in our brains. It is the essence of our being. We, humans, have the most evolved consciousness of all creatures. Consciousness is evolving with more and more features as we go higher and higher in evolutionary branches. If it is so, then it might have appeared at some point in the course of evolution.

Theory of evolution was proposed by Darwin. It says that about 4 billion years ago, a unique series of coincidental probabilities led to the existence of very simple biological cells that could replicate. These were the first forms of life. And as they replicated, subtle differences between the old cells and new cells would arise. Mutations would take place. We see it in the genetics of offspring of every life form known to us. All times the beneficial traits have been selected. Over billions of years of replicating and mutating, these biological mechanisms developed more and more sophisticated features in the organisms. Evolution has resulted, over millions of years of beneficial selection, extremely sophisticated human eye to emerge from origins as simplistic as a single light-sensitive protein molecule.

Therefore, it is tempting to think that this phenomenon of consciousness has emerged during the process of evolution. Just like every other feature of the human brain and body, experience or consciousness is a tool that evolution has engineered for us through billions of years of mutations. Conscious forms of life do have a higher capacity for learning and course-correcting. So evolution has selected this development and evolved it to a point where we became sentient and self-aware.

There are different opinions as to where in biological evolution, consciousness emerged. Some argue that we can date the origins of consciousness to the first animals with neurons and nervous systems.

Still, we should ask what that characteristic is that gives rise to the consciousness or subjective experiences out of this assembly of neurons.

Experiments at Vanderbilt University indicate that consciousness is an emergent property of the brain, resulting from more functional connectedness across all its regions spread over the whole brain and cannot be reduced to something residing in specific areas that control for qualities like attention, language, hearing, or memory.

Our experience of the world is unified. We experience a unified perception of visual and auditory cues. Therefore, the mechanism that widespread cross-network communication in the brain is giving rise to consciousness, which gives an integrated experience, seems sensible.

However, these brain states are just the correlations to experiential experiences. How they are causal to the first-person experiential description of consciousness is not explained.

Gerald Edelman and Giulio Tononi have proposed that re-entrant connections among the neurons that bi-directionally link areas of the brain in a massively parallel manner generate consciousness.

However here also, what physical laws are making the consciousness out of these complex patterns and organization of neurons in the brain and why it should be subjective, available to first-person only, is not explained.

The mind is viewed as an emergent property of the brain generated from and dependent upon the neural activity, but nonetheless separate from it. (TJ Voneida, 1998)

Saying that consciousness is an emergent phenomenon means physicalism. It means under certain pattern and organization of the brain matter, consciousness will emerge and it does not explain the hard problem of consciousness.

Moreover, consciousness as an evolutionary trait should be epiphenomenal, without influence on brain matter, quite like steam-whistle of a locomotive engine, which does not influence the machinery of the engine. It is argued that even this epiphenomenal consciousness confers beneficial advantages to species.

If the mind is emergent, it raises the difficulty for us having any free will.

Evolution in consciousness is limited by the evolution process of body plan and structure. Evolution of consciousness and evolution in physical body structure goes hand in hand, together.

Even if consciousness is proving to be of elusive nature to science, we need to make intelligent speculations, theories, explanations, and efforts to understand it.

Presently we are not able to make out as to how the consciousness could have been generating from the biological computations being performed in the assemblage of neurons in our brain but scientists are wary of conceptualising any kind of soul or spirit responsible for our consciousness. They maintain as we are able to explain all life processes like growth, metabolism, reproduction without requiring the need of any vital energy, so will be the case of consciousness. It will also be ultimately explained in terms of brain processes.

Philosophers have used an interesting thought experiment. We replace the hundred billion neurons of the brain by replicating silicon microchips one by one. Silicon chips are wired exactly the same way as neurons and they are wired up to your behaviour. Therefore, your behaviour will be exactly the same.

Then, will the silicon brain be conscious? One might think, only neurons can be conscious, silicon cannot be conscious.

As neurons are being replaced by silico-neurons, you observe if your consciousness fades away slowly and slowly or no effect. While replacing neurons by these silico-neurons you should be walking and talking exactly the same way.

If someone says that silicon cannot support consciousness, he has to say that somewhere along the way your consciousness suddenly disappears or fades out gradually. This may provide us good reason to believe that what really matters to consciousness are not neurons or silicons, the substrate brain matter that it is made of; what really matters is the organization, the dynamics of the underlying structures. It is the patterns, the organization, the information and not the specific structure of neurons or silicons or something else.

To explain the mechanism of consciousness, science says that it is an emergent phenomenon of the brain. The emergence of consciousness from the brain activity is analogous to the production of music from a record player. The music is not found anywhere inside the record player. The music is stored on the vinyl disc but we find only the peculiar grooves there. It is only through the mechanism of record player, the emergent phenomenon of music gets generated. Consciousness is somewhat similar. We can say that consciousness is generated by the brain. We cannot physically locate it at one point or in one area. Yet when billions of neurons fire and communicate with each other, the combination of the enormous amount of activity creates the phenomenon of consciousness.

Chapter 11

Plants are conscious

Nearly 99 per cent of all biomass on earth is in plants form. They look so different from the animals that have eyes and ears and have the movement that we often fail to notice that plants are also sentient beings.

The plant can sense, learn, remember, and even react in ways that humans know are the part of conscious behaviour of the animal world.

Plants do not have neurons or brains. 'Are plants conscious?' - This question was thought of by Charles Darwin also. He gave the concept of the root brain because the tips of the plant roots act as a kind of brain for them, accepting information from outside stimuli and telling the plant to act or to react.

Plants have the ability to sense and respond to stimuli. Plants respond to the stimuli of gravity, light, moisture, temperature, carbon-dioxide concentration, chemicals, parasites, and diseases. They can react to the stimuli of sound and touch.

Plants have certain photosensitive molecules like phototropin because of which they can sense light and respond as shoots grow towards sunlight and artificial light and roots usually grow away from light.

Plants roots grow towards gravity and shoots grow against gravity. The plant's gravity sensing cells are in the root tip and in the shoot tip which then distribute the plant growth hormone such that root grows towards gravity and shoot grows away from gravity. This plant movement under gravity is known as gravitropism.

When a tomato plant senses that a caterpillar is eating one of its leaves, it produces a kind of leaf toxin to repel the caterpillar.

In addition, the plant produces the hormone methyl jasmonate, which causes it to produce a volatile fragrance to alarm the neighbouring tomato plants, which detect the chemical and prepare for the attack by producing toxins that defend against insects. A little later, this plant produces a different scent that attracts the predators who may feed on these insets.

Tomato plant not only knows that it has been attacked but also who is attacking it. If the tomato is attacked by caterpillar, it produces one fragrance cocktail to attract parasitic wasps but if it is attacked by spider mite then it produces a different cocktail of fragrances to attract predatory mites. Probably plant is able to taste the saliva of insect and respond accordingly.

Plants throughout nature use this type of chemical signalling.

Mimosa plant is sensitive to touch. It closes down its leaves on the slightest touch. Carnivorous plant Venus flytrap snap shuts itself as the inset crawls inside its leaf. It will shut its leaf if the insect touches its cilia inside the leaf five times. This is taken as a sign that the plant is able to count also.

It is good for the static plant that it does not have a central brain system. What if its brain is chewed away by the insect? Otherwise, plants sense the stimuli from different sources and generate behavioural response suitable for integrated stimuli.

Because we tend to equate behaviour with mobility, we are not able to appreciate what plants can do. Because plants cannot run away and maybe get eaten, it is appropriate for them not to have any irreplaceable organs. A plant can lose up to ninety per cent of its body but may survive.

There are 20000 to 40000 and more genes in plants while there are only about 25000 genes in humans. It does not mean that plants are more conscious but shows plants are well adapted to their sessile life.

Formation of memories in plants

Plants can make memories. It has long been known that if you repeatedly touch a Mimosa plant it will stop folding its leaves, which is very much like the habituation learning in animals.

In 2014 Monica Gagliano & Team of the University of Western Australia decided to see if they could train a plant to change behaviour. If the plants were given the same stimulus over and over again, would it change its behaviour? Mimosa Pudica plant commonly known as 'touch-me-not' folds up its leaves if touched. Researchers, using a contraption, dropped the pot of the mimosa plant from a height. The plant folded its leaves on dropping. However, after 5-6 drops it stopped folding its leaves as if the plant has learnt that it was not going to harm and was not required of folding.

She checked up the plant by dropping after 28 days, the plant did not fold up its leaves. However, at the same time she shook away the plant, its leaves folded. The conclusion from the experiment is that mimosa plant could learn and that plant had formed long-lasting memory.

Biologists have shown that certain plants in certain situations can learn from their past experience and use it to guide how they grow or behave. They appear to be creating memories of drought exposure, cold or heat or poor soil.

A research group has shown that a plant may be forming an epigenetic memory of salt stress and pass it on to next generations also. However, as the stress factor goes away so does the memory.

In another experiment, Gagliano taught associative learning (Pavlonion conditioning) in garden pea plants. Here, in a Y shaped PVC pipe maze, the garden pea plants were kept. Plants natural response is to grow towards the light. In the experiment, she added another cue of airflow produced by a fan.

For some of the plants, light and air flowed from the same arm of the Y- maze. For others, light and airflow stimulus were made in opposite arms of the Y-maze so that light and airflow were in opposite directions for the plant.

For testing, the fan was switched on the opposite branch of the Y shape. The only stimulus present was airflow produced by the fan. The majority of the plants grew toward the fan if the fan was paired with light and away from the fan if the fan had been in opposite arm form the light.

Now the question arises who is doing the learning in plants? What could be actually happening when the association between fan and light stimulus are being made? Does it make sense to discuss learning and behaviour in plants with no neurons and no brain?

According to Gagliano, although the plants lack brains and neural tissues yet they do possess a sophisticated calcium-based signalling network in their cells similar to memory processes in animals.

Plants do not have a nervous system but produce some proteins found in animal neuron systems such as glutamate receptors and GABA receptors. Glutamate receptors in humans are used to form memories and several anaesthetics work through GABA receptors.

Plants are intelligent

Michael Pollan, an American journalist, writes in a New Yorker article that plants have ways of taking all the sensory data from its environment, integrate it, and behave in an appropriate way in response. Incredible thing is that they do it without brains and we assume that brains are needed to process information.

There is a video on YouTube of a talk given by Stefano Mancuso, plant neurobiologist from Italy titled

'Are plants conscious?' where he has presented a time-lapse video of bean plant searching for a metal pipe to climb. It seems there as if even before the plant reaches the pipe, the plant seems to know where the pipe is and try to wrap around it. In another case, one plant even seems to cede the pipe to another plant that pounds it first. These video footages are compelling and show lifelike intelligent behaviours in plants.

Intelligence means the ability to respond in an optimal way to the challenges presented by one's environment and circumstances. If we judge the behaviour of plants in the light of this definition of intelligence then we should be in no doubt that, plants are intelligent.

Damage or wound healing in plants

For animals or humans to feel pain, the nerves transmit an impulse to their brain where it is then interpreted as pain. Plants lack the nervous system or anything that can be said to be similar to it. Pain is a combination of physical damage and emotional distress. Plants do not seem to have anything like emotions.

Therefore, we can safely say that plants do not feel pain in a conventional way.

However, if pain means a response or reaction to damage then plants do have damage or wound healing system in response to damage.

To humans, pain is a useful tool. It indicates damage and allows us to respond accordingly. If we feel a headache, we need to respond by taking medicine or putting on the spectacles.

However, plants are rooted in the ground and they lack the mechanism to swat the insect away but it can release nasty or toxic chemicals to ward off the insect.

This release of chemicals is not a scream in pain but simply a reaction to damage quite like the response of our immune system.

Plants communicate, plants talk

Plants communicate with one another. They have social lives with other neighbouring plants. Plants communicate through volatile organic compounds above the ground and they communicate stress signals via their roots.

Aphid infested bean plants release volatile fragrances into the air to warn their neighbouring bean plants. They respond by releasing different fragrance cocktail to repel the aphids and to attract the aphid eating wasps.

The roots of most plants are connected through the fungal network in the soil. These fungi meet the need of the mineral nutrients of plants in exchange for carbon. Plants send warning signals through these roots connected through mycelium network.

Plants signalling with one another are part of plants communication and cooperation with one another in their neighbourhood.

Professor Ariel Novoplansky at Ben-Gurion University, Israel and team did a study as to show that the drought stress signals are communicated through the roots of the plants.

Novoplansky's team planted the pea plants in six pots, such that, each pot contained the roots of two different plants. Then, they subject the first plant in the row to drought-like condition. The first plant closed its stomata on leaf surfaces in response to drought stress.

It was found that after some time the adjacent plant had closed its stomata. Even the unstressed neighbour plants have closed their stomata after some more time. Then they did the experiment with different plants in different pots so that now the roots were not in contact. The first plant was put in drought stress conditions. It closed its stomata but the neighbouring plants in different pots did not close their stomata.

It was made clear that the drought stress signal was communicating to the neighbouring plants through the roots. The drought stress cue is of chemical nature mainly. When researchers took the soluble chemicals, extracted from the soil of the drought-stressed plant, and used that to unstressed plants roots, they found that this unstressed plant responded in the same way as a stressed plant.

Plants sense sounds also

When certain sounds are played to the roots at the corn plants, their roots bend towards the source of the sound.

Monica Gagliano suggests besides the airborne volatiles and roots communication through soluble chemicals or through the common fungal network, plants may also be using sound as communication means.

Monica Gagliano did yet another experiment on chilli seeds. When Chilli seeds were grown where they were exposed to fennel plant, they germinated more slowly. The fennel plant is a dominant plant that releases chemicals into the air and soil that slow other plants growth.

However, when the chilli seeds were grown beside the sealed off fennel such that there could not have been any chemical signalling or optical signalling through air or soil, chilli seeds sprouted very fast; as if they were yet sensing a signal of some sort.

In a separate set up, chilli seeds growing next to a sealed-off chilli plant also grew differently than they would have grown isolated, suggesting some form of signalling between the two.

What kind of signalling might be at work in these cases? Gagliano suggests that there could be sound-based signals.

The experiments done by Appel and Cocroft in 2014 found that even when the recordings of the munching noise produced by caterpillar are played back to the plants, plants responded by releasing the defensive chemicals in its leaves to ward off the caterpillar.

Plants show social life

Kin recognition is important in social systems. In 2007, Susan A Dudley and Amanda L File in a study made on the beach weed, also called sea rocket, demonstrated that the allocation to roots increased when a group of strangers shared a common pot, but it was normal when a group of siblings shared a pot. Less competition in roots growth is indicative of kin selection.

Plants are affected by anaesthetics

Plants get sedated by human anaesthetics. Plants produce their own compounds that are anaesthetics to us.

A study by K Yokawa and team published in Annals of Botany (2017) shows that anaesthetics affect plants as well.

Mimosa leaves, pea tendrils and Venus flytraps reversibly lose their autonomous movements and touch induced movements after exposure to anaesthetics. Under diethyl ether anaesthetics, Venus flytrap does not shut down its leaves to trap the insect even if the insect passes through its leaves.

After being exposed to diethyl ether vapour, pea tendrils stop moving and curl up.

After exposure to anaesthesia, the seedlings stayed dormant and germination is impeded.

It was shown that after one hour of 15% diethyl ether vapour treatment to Mimosa Plants the plants completely lost their response to touch stimuli. The response recovered after 7 hours of the removal of diethyl ether.

The venues flytrap showed a similar effect on the application of 15% diethyl ether for an hour. Multiple stimulations to its trigger hairs did not close its trap. The response recovered 15 minutes after the removal of diethyl ether. During anaesthesia, they did not produce the electrical signals.

Another carnivorous plant sundew, which captures prey through its sticky tentacles on leaves, also lost its ability to bend their tentacles and leaves when exposed to diethyl ether.

When the anaesthesia wore off, the plants came back to life. As if, anaesthesia hit the pause button in them. As if the plants lost their consciousness, and when anaesthetic effects wore off, the plants regained their consciousness.

It appears that in plants anaesthetics affect the physical properties of the cell membrane. The transportation of cellular material across the membrane becomes difficult. Plant cells electrical activity, which transfers messages across membranes from one cell to another that leads to movement or action, seems to be disrupted by anaesthetics in plants.

The membrane becomes more flexible. If we apply pressure to cells, the anaesthetic effect wears off.

Plants and animals have similar life mechanisms

The plants and animals evolved separately about 1.6 billion years ago from their last common ancestor. Plants and animals both are eukaryotic cells.

They use the same enzymes to replicate their DNA and have the same types of ribosome to make proteins. Their cells have nuclei and genes are packed in chromosomes. Both have cell cytoskeleton of microtubules and have mitochondria. Energy producing mechanism is also the same in both the cells. As animals have evolved since then to produce humans in animal's lineage, the same kind of evolution would have produced quite complex mechanisms in plants world also.

The mechanisms in plant and animal world are so similar that genes from the animal can be put in plants and they further produce the functional proteins. For example, planting the jellyfish genes in a tomato plant can make the tomato glow in the dark.

If one looks at the biochemistry and cell structure of animals and plants, then it becomes obvious that they should have evolved from a common ancestor cell.

But is this consciousness?

Plants do not have the sensory organs like eyes, ears, or noses but plants have developed their own methods to sense potential threats around them. Plants do have their own resistance to pathogens and have means to withstand the different stresses like heat, drought, salinity, or cold.

How the humble plants are able to sense their environment is not fully known but the progress is being made in knowing the cues available and given by plants in their environment. However, even the known facts about them are sufficient to make us in wonder that depth of intelligent life on earth spreads to plants as well.

Plants have electrical and chemical signalling systems, shows learning and memory. They seem to communicate alarm signals, stress factors to its neighbours, gets sedated by anaesthesia. All this behaviour is so lifelike.

Therefore, we can safely say that Plants are as alive as animals and as humans.

Moreover, why should not we extend ourselves to think that plants are also having consciousness quite like animals and humans? In all probability, plants are conscious and sentient creations.

Chapter 12

Theories of consciousness-Global Workspace Theory and Integrated Information Theory

Consciousness is the subjective experience we have associated with any observation, we make. We have the mental imagery somewhere on a projected screen through our minds and having view and having the inner voice. There is a difficulty to comprehend as to how the subjective experience is resulting out of the physical matter of the brain.

The dominant view is that the mind or consciousness is the construct of the brain somehow; however, some thinkers still support that mind is separate from the material body.

Neuroscientists have also come forward and provided theories to explain consciousness. Two of the promising theories have been summarized here.

Global Workspace Theory

The global workspace theory of consciousness was proposed in its elementary framework by a neuroscientist Bernard Baars in 1983. Since that time, there have been many modifications of the theory but the central theme has always been that when information is available in the brain globally, it gives rise to conscious awareness of the information.

In the brain, we have distributed modules (specialists) which are dedicated to various special functions and they have a fleeting working memory. These specialists are continuously processing information on their own, independent of the functions of other modules. Various unconscious processes are occurring in the brain at any time.

The fleeting memory holds the content of only one information processing event at a time.

The role of consciousness is to decide the dominant context from amongst the many information processing events in various specialists fleeting memories. Then, there happens attentional amplification.

Attentional amplification causes the contents of this dominant working memory to be broadcasted to the whole of the brain system, which makes us become aware of, or conscious of this content. There is evidence that, as predicted by Global Workspace Theory, conscious experience of visual contents evokes highly distributive activity in non-visual regions of the brain.

Experimental support for Global workspace theory

If the consciousness arises from a dedicated brain area or a 'seat of consciousness' was responsible for our subjective conscious experiences or if consciousness was the result of concerted, coordinated activity across the entire brain-

to probe these questions we have to look into the brain processes for which non-invasive techniques such as magnetic resonance imaging and EEG may not be quite useful as they give either spatial or temporal information but not both. The best way to get both spatial and temporal information simultaneously is to implant electrodes deep inside the skull but it could be done only in cases of epilepsy patients who needed to undergo surgical procedures.

Neuroscientists Raphael Gaillard and the team of INSERM in Gif Sur Yvette, France got an opportunity to probe consciousness in 10 people who had electrodes implanted in their brains for treating drug-resistant epilepsy.

Gaillard's team, for their research, flashed some words before the volunteers for a very short period and also used visual masks so that the words were either consciously processed or processed only unconsciously while they monitored signals from the electrodes. They found that during the first 300 ms of the experiment, brain activity during both the non-conscious and conscious processing was very similar, indicating that the process of consciousness had not kicked in. But after that, there were several types of brain activity, showing distinct neurophysiological markers that only occurred in the individuals who were aware of the words.

Firstly, there was an increase in the voltage levels of the signals in their brains. Secondly, the frequency and phase of neurons firing in different parts of the brain tended to synchronize. Then some of these synchronized signals appeared to be triggering other regions. Thus the conscious awareness of the word triggered the activity spread across the brain. For example, activity in the occipital lobe seemed to cause activity in the frontal lobe.

Galliard team says that because this activity only occurred in those volunteers who were aware of the words, this constitutes a consciousness signature, and consciousness does not have a single seat. Consciousness is more of a coordinated activity across wide area of the brain rather than a local activity.

Bernard Baars says that this provides strong evidence for his Global Workspace Theory of consciousness.

Now the signatures of consciousness have also been found in brain scans

Aaron Schurger of Princeton University in New Jersey and his team in 2009 used the idea of a reproducibility measure to differentiate conscious and non-conscious processes. The team thought that if same sensory input, say a picture, was made to process consciously each time, it should have produced the similar replicating neural patterns in fMRI brain scans, which would give them clues as to what consciousness was.

They found that brain scans show the similar pattern of neural activity each time the same image is processed consciously but the neural patterns were much more variable when the image processed in the brain unconsciously because many different subconscious activities would have been processing.

These patterns of brain activity in non-invasive brain scans can help in determining if the patients with brain damage are still conscious or not. These consciousness signatures can also be helpful to probe consciousness in animals.

Integrated Information Theory

Integrated Information Theory (IIT) is a mathematical framework proposed by neuroscientist Giulio Tononi in 2004 to explain what consciousness is and why it might be associated with certain physical systems. Tononi's integrated information theory of consciousness is a non-reductionist theory; it does not reduce consciousness but assumes it and connects it to physical processes.

The theory starts with the presumption that consciousness exists. Tononi explains that consciousness means our experiences- experiences we feel of shapes or sounds, thoughts or emotions about the world or about the self and theory presumes 'I experience, therefore, I am'.

It postulates that experience is structured and has multiple aspects in various combinations. A visual experience of a blue book has aspects of shape (book) and colour (blue). Experiences are integrated means like a word 'best' written in red ink at the centre of the page cannot be seen independent of its colour red or 'be' on the left and 'st' on right. Every experience will have different information contents.

And, then, it goes on to look into the physical substrate, that is, neurons and brain and what it could be in the brain that is giving rise to the consciousness.

A physical system is a set of elements like neurons or logic gates, which are in a particular state. The element in a state has the cause-effect power upon itself. States of the system in the past are the causes and produces the future states, effects.

The element of the system generates information if its past state makes a difference to the present state of the element and its present state makes a difference to the future state.

Elementary systems can form higher-order systems in various combinations.

The combinations of elementary systems generate integrated information, which cannot be reduced to further independent components. This integrated information is quantified by Φ (phi), consciousness factor, a measure of the difference D between the information specified by the whole and the product of the information as specified by the partitioned independent components.

Integrated information is about only one set, out of all possible values of causes and effects, which has a maximally irreducible cause-effect structure. This maximum corresponds to the conscious state and corresponding consciousness factor Φ can be approximated by the mathematical formula set out in theory. The experience is the set of all such maxima of different modules of the brain, which is called the maximally irreducible conceptual structure.

According to IIT, consciousness requires a grouping of elements that may be neurons or logic gates or others, within a system that are connected in re-entrant architecture consisting of feedback loops. The human brain or the part of it, the cerebrum, that supports our consciousness has very high Φ and is therefore highly conscious. It has all kinds of experiences. Systems with low Φ will have a small amount of consciousness, they can have very minimal experiences. Systems with zero Φ are not conscious at all.

It is not an identity between the experience and its physical substrate, the elements, as such, but is an identity between an experience and maximally irreducible conceptual structure as specified by a set of elements in a state. The quality of experience, the level to which it exists, is given by its irreducibility.

Computer and internet are not conscious

We may ask why brains are conscious while computers are not. A computer can have as much information as a brain and behaviourally can be as self-determining. However, in a computer, every transistor is connected to only a few other transistors. Its structural features are its modularity and feedforward connectivity. Therefore, computers have very low integrated information, Φ.

Internet is a highly integrated form of node point computers for the purpose of point-to-point communication. It can also be used to broadcast messages from any one node to many others. Yet it seems unlikely that at least in its current form the internet is giving rise to some kind of globally integrated consciousness. What could be the critical difference between the network of neurons inside the brain that gives rise to human consciousness and the network of internet routers connecting devices throughout the worlds?

Tononi says that the critical difference is that the neural substrate of consciousness is wired to achieve maxima of integrated information whereas the internet just ensures point-to-point communication and it is not designed to achieve a maximum of integrated information.

Exclusion postulate of IIT

By contrast, within consciousness, every experience is the entire set of concepts that make up any particular experience as to what it is and what it is not and are maximally integrated. But this maximal information integration also causes exclusion. One does not become conscious of what is going on within the modules in his brain like the module that performs language parsing. He hears and understands an English sentence but has no conscious access to how the relevant parts of his brain are achieving this computation. According to IIT, many components of the brain like amygdala or visual cortex may have non-zero phi and hence may qualify to be called mini minds. However, because the phi of the entire brain exceeds that of its mini components, its consciousness excludes the component 'mini minds'.

Low interconnection or low information means low consciousness

Our consciousness depends on the cerebral cortex or say cerebrum. Lesions and damage to cerebral cortex affect person's consciousness whereas the complete removal of the cerebellum, which has four times, the number of neurons than in cerebrum and which is important for motor functions and balance hardly affects consciousness. According to IIT, more neurons mean more information but not more integration. In the cerebellum, neurons are far less interconnected than the cerebrum. So cerebrum, being highly interconnected, gives rise to the rich experience of consciousness, whereas, cerebellum does not support consciousness.

The degree of consciousness does not correspond to the degree of brain activity. During epileptic seizures, brain activity is increased but it may lose consciousness. Cortical neurons remain active throughout sleep, but their firing patterns change. So at certain times during deep sleep consciousness fades while at other times we may dream. These patterns of brain activity may be resulting in low information or low integration making our brain states of overall low consciousness.

Calculation of Φ

In integrated information theory, we can in principle measure the consciousness of any system by calculating its Φ. But calculations for Φ becomes very complicated even for the simple systems. But Many shortcuts and assumptions can be used to have an approximate idea of Φ for the systems.

Explaining binding in IIT

Theories of consciousness need to account for the binding problem. The different elements of a simple experience of viewing have characteristics like colour, shape, or orientation, which are processed by a different set of neurons in the brain, yet they provide one whole experience of viewing the object. Any theory of consciousness will have to account as to how this is happening. IIT accounts it by describing the conceptual structure, which is set off all concepts specified by a group of elements in a state with their respective Φ max values.

IIT endorse panpsychism

In IIT, consciousness is identified with the physical integration of information systems. Consciousness is fundamental to these systems in the same way as mass or charge or spin is basic to certain particles. IIT can apply to all forms of matter provided the systems made in it have elements that output feedback into its input stages.

Panpsychism doctrine holds that consciousness is a property not just of brains but it exists in all matter even in table or chair. IIT applies not only to the neuronal matter of brains but it applies to all forms of matter and it implies that panpsychism might be true. Even a proton, which forms from the interconnection of quarks, may have non-zero phi and so may be conscious.

Criticism of IIT

Christof Koch, a neuroscientist, supports IIT as a really promising fundamental theory of consciousness.

How does the physical matter of our brains make the mind? How it becomes conscious and generates subjective experiences like those as you are reading these sentences? How can physical matter in whatever form or format account for our subjective experiences, which is known as the hard problem of consciousness as espoused by philosopher David Chalmers? IIT does not solve the hard problem of consciousness.

Scott Aaronson, an American computer scientist, criticizes IIT that a two-dimensional grid can be made in logic gates, which will have very high Φ measure. But it does not look like that they will seem to be conscious at all.

Philosopher John Searle has criticized IIT that its explanation of consciousness is based on some pattern of information while information presupposes consciousness. There are all types of information in books, computers, and hard drives but this information makes sense only relative to our capacity to interpret them. Therefore, consciousness cannot be explained by saying that it is consisted of information. Information based theories of consciousness are circular.

But this theory under development since 2004, proposed and advanced by neuroscientists makes one thing clear that even neuroscientists think that there is a need to account for subjective conscious experience also known as consciousness in popular problem literature. They want to move beyond their explanation of consciousness as one's observed behaviour and the details of his brain organization.

J. Horgan, an American science Journalist writes, "Pondering IIT has deepened my appreciation of the mind-body problem. In an age of rampant scientism, we need theories like IIT to help us rediscover the mystery of ourselves- in that sense, they work".

Chapter 13

Placebo effect, Acupuncture, Homeopathy

Placebo effect

Placebo effect is a really remarkable phenomenon. Placebo is basically a fake treatment, a fake medicine. Placebo is an inactive substance like a sugar pill, distilled water or saline solution instead of medicine but that can sometimes improve a patient's medical condition simply because the person has the expectation that it will be helpful. The placebo effect is the reported improvement in the feel of a medical condition by a patient. Placebo can even be a fake surgery.

Most of the clinical trials of the medicines done by pharmaceutical companies are compared to a control group who is given placebo treatment. If the medicine is more effective in improving the medical condition of the patient than the placebo, a nothing, then medicine is said to be of therapeutic value. Sometimes placebo effect, the improvement in symptoms of the medical condition on taking the fake drug, is also compared to a third control group who is given no treatment.

The placebo effect is psychological as well as physiological

One of the most common theories of why the placebo effect happens is that the placebo effect happens due to the person's expectations. If a person expects that taking the pill would be beneficial then expectation can modulate the body's own chemistry such that it can cause effects, similar to what a medication might have caused.

Placebo effect seems to be a psychological phenomenon where despite the inert ingredients of the dummy pill, your mind acts as a powerful healing tool. Improved outcomes reported by the patients on taking the placebo are due to their subjective perceptions as well as due to physiological effects.

Placebo effect and understanding of its underlying neurobiological mechanisms can throw us some new light on mind-body interaction. The mental events in placebo effect activate mechanisms that are similar to those activated by drugs. Placebo administration indicates a link between psychological and pharmacodynamic effects.

Painkilling and anxiety-reducing actual medicines, if given without the knowledge of the patient, they are effective. However, when the patient knows that he is receiving such medicine, its therapeutic effect is more.

Research studies in placebo phenomenon

In a study conducted by Ted Kaptchuk of Harvard Medical School in 2010, it was found that placebo worked even when the patients knew that they had received a dummy pill. Eighty patients suffering from irritable bowel syndrome (IBS) were divided into two groups. One group, the controls, received no treatment while the other group received a placebo. It was told to them that the pills had no active ingredient and were made from inert substances but were also told that sometimes placebos were effective. The patients receiving placebo reported adequate symptom relief. It seemed to work for many of them.

In Cochrane systematic review involving the use of placebo published in 2004, it was found that placebo treatment caused no major health benefit as it did not affect the illness clinically although the patients receiving the placebo reported the improved outcome as they had improved perception of nausea and pain.

However, another review study done by J. Howick and team in 2013, found that placebo and treatments had similar effects.

There also happens 'nocebo effect' when the patient receiving a placebo reports negative effect i.e. worsening of symptoms. Nocebo effect can cause side effects like headache, nausea, or dizziness associated with real treatment. A nocebo effect may occur when the patient has negative expectations regarding treatment.

Counselling given by the Doctor has a great bearing on therapeutic effect irrespective of any treatment. Counselling influences the patient's expectations about the illness or the treatment through positive information about the treatment or the illness.

Placebo pill and counselling do not have a direct physiological effect. However, seem to affect the health outcomes through indirect effects.

In one study, placebo was given as a stimulant. Their pulse rate increased and blood pressure increased. When the same pill was given but told that it would help them to sleep, they experienced the opposite effect.

However, in one study done on asthma patients, it was found that placebo administration did not affect the illness per se but the patients still reported subjective improvements.

Some studies have found that placebo administration increases the body's production of endorphins, one of the body's natural pain relievers while placebo motor improvement is mediated by the body's production of dopamine.

A review study done by brain imaging techniques on placebo phenomenon by V. Faria and team in 2008 found that imaging studies show evidence of specific, predictable, and replicable patterns of neural activities associated with placebo administration. In general, placebo responses seem mediated by frontal cortical areas that generate and maintain cognitive expectancies.

One study by Kathryn hall and team in 2012 suggested that genes might also influence how people responded to placebo treatments. The study found that the people who had high dopamine variant of the gene that controls dopamine levels in the prefrontal cortex of the brain were more likely to respond to placebo treatment than those with low dopamine variation of the same gene.

A research carried out by Eippert and team from Germany in 2009 suggests that the placebo effect works by reduced pain signalling from the spinal cord to the brain.

During the research study, the spinal cords of 15 healthy volunteers were scanned. During the scan, they received laser pinpricks to their hands. An inactive cream was applied on the hand but some of them were told that the pain-relieving cream had been applied. The volunteers who were told that pain relief cream was applied reported feeling less pain and their scans showed significantly reduced activity in the spinal cord pathways.

Placebo is a powerful phenomenon

The overall placebo effect is a very profound thing. This shows how psychological factors can influence the subjective perception of pain feelings. In addition, the subjective experience of feeling better is due to objective measurable changes in brain chemistry.

Earlier placebo was defined as any medicine adapted more to please than to benefit the patient. Many times doctors prescribe antibiotics for viral illness and vitamins for fatigue as a measure of placebo only, more to calm the patient rather than actual benefits in those cases.

Placebos and their effects cannot be dismissed out of hand. Placebos have been shown to work in the number of situations.

Robert Buckman, a clinical oncologist and professor of medicine from Canada, had said, "Placebos are extra-ordinary drugs. They seem to have some effect on almost every symptom known to humankind and work in, at least, a third of patients and sometimes in up to 60 per cent. They have no serious side effects and cannot be given in overdose. In short, they hold the prize for the most adaptable, protean, effective, safe and cheap drugs in the world's pharmacopeia."

Acupuncture

Acupuncture has been a traditional Chinese therapy that is clinically practised the world over. Acupuncture involves stimulation of acupuncture points by penetration of the skin with very thin needles. Sometimes a low-frequency current may also be applied to the needles to provide greater stimulation.

Acupuncture theory says that the body's vital energy known as 'qi' or 'chi' circulates through channels called meridians and they have branches connected to body organs and functions. The illness is caused by the disruptions to the flow of energy in the body. Acupuncture may, in theory, correct imbalances of this energy flow at acupuncture points close to the skin.

Acupuncture theory has not found any backing of anatomy or physiology. There are no corresponding biomedical or physical features in the body corresponding to the qi meridians and acupuncture points.

Many studies have been conducted to find if the acupuncture is really effective. The results have been inconsistent. Some research results suggest that acupuncture can bring relief in pain but the majority of the research suggests that benefits of acupuncture are mainly due to placebo effect. Even if needles are inserted at wrong places or sham needles are used where no actual needle insertion takes place, are equally effective.

Acupuncture should generally be done by a trained person using sterile single-use needles. Acupuncture if done in poor hygiene conditions may result in bacterial infections at the site of needle insertions. Even the injuries like an accidental puncture of the lung have been reported.

Homeopathy

Homeopathy is an alternative medicine, which originated in Germany and is used all over the world. This was started by Samuel Hahnemann. It is based on the principle 'like cures like' that means a substance that caused disease in the first place in healthy people would cure symptoms in sick people if given in minute doses.

Homeopathy medicines are prepared by diluting the active ingredient in water or alcohol and it is diluted to that extent that there remains almost no trace of it. The proponents of homeopathy practice claim that the properties of the ingredient get trapped in water that remains beneficial even if there is no trace of the active ingredient in the diluted form.

In its principle like cures like is the idea that the substance in minute doses may stimulate the immune system of the body itself and help it to heal.

In homeopathy practice, the doctor interviews the patient to get a thorough idea of a patient's medical history and symptoms, both physical and emotional. The idea is to learn about the patient to help him holistically, in the most effective way possible.

A 2015 Australian report of Australian National Health and Medical Research Council of Homeopathy, which considered the results of many studies on the effectiveness of homeopathy, is relevant. It concluded that homeopathy remedies are no better than a sugar pill, a placebo. There are no health conditions for which there is reliable evidence that homeopathy is effective.

Chapter 14

Organ transplantation, Cryopreservation, Cryptobiosis

Organ transplantation

An organism is an individual entity that exhibits the properties of life like reproduction, growth, and development, response to stimuli and maintenance.

Organisms can be unicellular like bacteria or can be multicellular composed of trillions of cells like humans. Multicellular animals have specialised tissues and organs that have specialized functions.

In case an organ becomes dysfunctional, we may require replacing this organ with a healthy organ. Organ transplantation is done from the donor body to recipient body in case of severe organ failure. We see the increase in success rates due to improvement in surgical methods, organ preservation, and immunological therapies.

While organs and tissue donations can be done after the donor has died but some organs like kidney, part of the liver or lung or tissues are also donated while the donor is alive. There are about as many living donors as there are deceased donors.

Here we try to look at the field of organ transplantation from the point of view of how long the organ can be alive outside the body before transplantation.

As the organ is removed from the donor, the organ is flushed free of blood with an ice-cold perseveration solution that contains electrolytes and nutrients. The removed organ is then placed in a sterile container, which is kept in ice. Thereafter the organ is maintained in cold state and transported to the hospital where it is to be transplanted in a recipient's body.

Bone and skin can survive as long as 8 to 12 hours. Heart valves and corneas can be donated within the first 24 hours of death.

The eyes of a dead person can be used only if they are removed within six hrs of death.

The kidney can be transplanted in the recipient's body within 24 hours after removing from donor's body.

Once the donor's liver is removed, it needs to be transplanted in the recipient's body within six hours.

The brain does not recover after more than 3 minutes of stoppage of blood circulation. Generally, as a rule, it can be considered that brain cells begin to die after approximately 4 to 6 minutes of no blood flow. After around 10 minutes, those cells will cease functioning and the brain would become dead.

Hearing is the last sense to go in the dying process. Talking to a person who is ill is a very effective therapy itself.

After removal of the heart from the brain dead donor's body, a heart can survive just about four hours. It would need to be transplanted within this time period.

If there is no blood flow to the heart muscles within 20-40 minutes, irreversible death of the muscle will begin to occur.

Organs and tissues can be transplanted until the time they are alive. Their period of aliveness is increased by keeping them in ice, cold conditions and often a preserving solution is used.

Recently the scientists in Sweden have made a heart safe box to keep the heart alive for transplantation outside the body. The device is able to extend the time between heart donation and transplantation from four hours to more than 12 hours.

The device is a mini-heart lung machine, which provides the donated heart with an oxygenated solution containing vital nutrients. The device was able to keep the animal heart alive for up to 24 hours.

It is possible similar devices for other organs are also made.

In regenerative medicine, we use stem cells or progenitor cells obtained through directed differentiation to restore normal function of the organs in the body. It avoids the problem of rejection because patients own cells are used.

In tissue engineering, we use cells or a combination of cells generally around a scaffold of biomaterial capable of supporting three-dimensional tissue formations. The cells grow into the tissues around the scaffold in a culture medium that are used for medical purposes.

Cells, tissues, and organs can live outside the body independent of the body under suitable conditions. They can be alive outside the body and can be transplanted again in the body where they get integrated again with the live body of the recipient.

In one of the news, Yale University neuroscientist Nenad Sestan told that the pig's brain has been kept alive for 36 hours as a standalone with a system of pumps, heaters, and bags of artificial blood warmed to body temperature. They found billions of active healthy brain cells within that brain. There was no electrical activity between brain cells, just a flat brain wave. That animal brain is not aware of anything. The brain may not have been conscious but the cells were alive. If the cells are alive, it is a living organ.

However, brain transplantation has not yet been achieved.

The sense of self and the personality of the recipient do not change if the heart is transplanted. The recipient will feel the same self and the same personality as before the transplant, except maybe the quality of life, has improved for him.

It is possible for the cells taken from the organs to survive and grow independently under the proper culture conditions.

Sub-cell structures like organelles also can temporarily survive and function outside the cell under suitable culture medium.

Proteins are the workhorses in the cell functioning. Scientists have been able to improve or block their functioning with the help of drugs within the cell but they are not stable outside the body. In order to fulfil their specialized functions within the cell, proteins are folded into very precise structures. Outside of the body, they fall apart quickly.

Genome sequencing pioneer Craig Venter and Den Gibson synthesized the chromosome chemically and transplanted that into a cell to make a synthetic bacterium which was capable of self-replicating.

Polymerase Chain Reaction (PCR) is a method for selective replication of specific DNA and RNA sequences outside the cell environment.

In vitro fertilization (IVF) technique allows the sperm to fertilize an egg in a culture dish and implanting the resulting embryo into the uterus.

In a bid to know about life and its complexity, an artificial cell is being tried to be created from the individual cell components in a bottom-up approach.

It seems the synthesis of living life is not an unrealistic goal for the advancing steps of man.

Brain Death

In brain death patients, complete loss of brain function including the brain stem function, happens. Autonomic respiration activity ceases. However, respiration can be maintained by mechanical ventilation. There is a total lack of electrical activity in the brain as seen in electroencephalograph EEGs taken at an interval of 12 to 24 hours.

If the brain stem is still functioning then heartbeat and ventilation can still be there, unaided. However, in brain dead people where the brain stem is also dead, immediately after the brain death, the heart's intrinsic electrical system will keep the organ beating for a short time. It will also be dead if oxygen is not provided. Its spontaneous breathing stops. Therefore, a mechanical ventilator has to be connected to keep the breathing going and the heart and body getting the oxygen.

With just a ventilator, biological processes like kidney and digestive function can continue for about a week.

Without the brain, important hormones are not secreted, so the biological process like kidney functions and digestive functions are difficult to keep running for longer than a week.

Without the brain, normal blood pressure, which is also critical for bodily functions often, cannot be maintained without blood pressure medication.

A brain dead person cannot maintain homeostasis i.e. body temperature cannot so be maintained so warm IV fluids are required to keep the body warm.

The body of the brain-dead persons can be kept alive for days together, without blood flow to the brain, with the support of ventilators, hormones, blood pressure medication and warm IV fluid etc. but the person has lost so-called consciousness irreversibly.

Generally, the family of the brain dead person is coaxed to donate the organs.

Can characteristic of being alive be independent of the characteristic of being conscious? Biological death is when the brain, as well as body, is dead and no longer alive. Should we search for the consciousness in the condition of being alive itself?

Cryopreservation

Cryopreservation is the process of freezing the biological material like cells, sperms, eggs, embryos, tissues, organs for their preservation at the temperatures of -196°C with liquid nitrogen.

At these low temperatures, any enzymatic or chemical reactions in the cells are effectively stopped, including the biochemical reactions that lead to cell death and DNA degradation.

Therefore, this preservation method makes it possible to store living cells without damage to them for years, decades, and centuries. Cryopreservation techniques include thawing back the cells back to functional conditions.

The critical issue in cryopreservation is to prevent intracellular ice formation to keep the cell membrane intact and cells alive. Another issue of concern is the toxicity of the cryoprotectant solution.

There are two main methods for cryopreservation-

Slow freezing

In the slow freezing process, for example, embryo preservation involves bathing an embryo (usually of three to five days after fertilization) in a cryoprotectant solution of anti-freeze compounds like glycerol or dimethyl sulphoxide. The solution draws moisture out of the embryo and cryoprotectant works its way into the cells, which prevent ice crystals from forming inside the cell. Freezing rate is kept around 1°C/minute.

When the temperature reaches -30°C to -40°C, it is then directly freezed and stored in liquid nitrogen solution (-196°C).

For implanting the embryo, the thawing process is done. It involves soaking the embryo in a warm bath that gradually washes away the cryoprotectant solution.

Vitrification

Instead of a slow freeze method, we can use the vitrification process for cryopreservation.

Vitrification is an ultra-rapid cooling process. Here the cooling rates are of thousands of degrees per minute.

Here, the embryos are exposed to 5-10 times more cryoprotectant solution than slow freeze process. Then, they are directly dipped into liquid nitrogen of -196°C.

The rapid cooling and high cryoprotectant inside allows the cell contents to turn into a glass-like substance instead of ice.

Vitrification process stops the cell biology and cells can be preserved for long times.

Cryptobiosis and the Limits of Life

In nature, we can look at certain organisms that undergo cryptobiosis to know the limits of life.

Cryptobiosis (hidden life) as defined by David Keilin is "the state of an organism when it shows no visible signs of life and when its metabolic activity becomes hardly measurable or comes reversibly to a standstill."

Certain organisms, in situations of adverse environmental conditions such as extreme dryness, extreme cold, and oxygen deficiency, can enter into a cryptobiotic state of life where their metabolic activity comes to a halt yet they are not dead. When environmental conditions become hospitable again, these organisms can return back to their normal life.

Anhydrobiosis is a form of cryptobiosis, which occurs in situations of extreme desiccation. It means life without water. Certain animals such as tardigrades or water bears, rotifers, brine shrimp or sea monkeys, nematodes are adapted to anhydrobiosis. Majority of plant seeds, resurrection plant, and certain microorganisms like baker's yeast also exhibit anhydrobiotic forms of life. In the anhydrobiotic state, organisms can survive for decades.

Tardigrade releases up to 95 per cent of its free and stored water and forms trehalose sugar in its body, thus entering into a contracted body called a tun, an almost completely desiccated state, which stabilises its membrane and other structures while maintaining their spatial arrangement. Trehalose sugar might be serving as a water substitute. Trehalose form amorphous glass, a highly viscous biomolecules matrix at low water content along with macro-molecules and metabolites (vitrification) thus preserving their spatial arrangement and halting their motion.

Tardigrade can withstand extreme temperature, radiation and pressure while in a cryptobiotic state.

In the situation of lack of or absence of oxygen (anoxia), tardigrades take in water and become turgid and immobile, but they enter into a state of inactivity and can survive for long periods of time. Metabolic activity is hardly measurable if not standstill in this state of cryptobiosis called anoxybiosis. However, the biological feasibility of inactive state of anoxybiosis wherein an organism is able to preserve its biological structures despite the abundance of water and thermal energy is inconclusive. However, brine shrimp, copepods, nematodes, and sponge gemmules are capable of successfully surviving in a seemingly inactive state during the absence of oxygen for periods of 3 months to years.

Since the extremities help us in defining rules so, it is useful to know the limits of life.

Chapter 15
Artificial intelligence and consciousness

Artificial intelligence (AI) based systems are primarily based on the information processing models of human intelligence and thinking in which the analogy of the brain as a computer is taken quite literally.

One of the practical goals of AI is to implement aspects of human intelligence in computers. Human intelligence is best viewed as intelligence capable of higher-order thinking skills like use of language, problem solving, analysis, evaluation, creative generation, logical reasoning, planning and critical thinking etc. In computer modelling of these levels of intelligence, we may need to create structural hierarchies of more basic levels of intelligence models.

Another approach can be that we simulate the human brain as interconnections of elemental neural network models to create the desired mental and behavioural outcomes.

We have succeeded in creating many artificial intelligent systems like expert systems, speech recognition, machine vision, self-driving cars etc. We are steadily advancing in creating intelligent machines in computers and robots that work and react like intelligent humans and other animals.

The brain is not a CPU. Neurons in the brain do not have an algorithm, which is run in the CPU of the brain. brain as a computer is, in fact, a poor analogy. In AI, we are working on big data so that the computer can be made to understand its world around itself and behave in an optimal manner.

There is a group of scientists like Ray Kurzweil, an American computer expert, who believes that a sufficiently advanced artificial intelligence system may become conscious. As of now, artificial systems do not appear to be conscious. Consciousness is the subjective experience associated with perceptions.

John Searle, professor of philosophy at the University of California, Berkley says that we have no idea how the brain produces consciousness. Computation is not a fact of nature; it is a fact of our interpretation. We have created artificial machines that carry out computations but the computation by itself is never going to be sufficient for thinking or understanding because the computation is defined purely formally or syntactically. His famous thought experiment 'Chinese Room' shows that a computer answering in Chinese to the questions put to it in Chinese does not, in fact, 'understand' Chinese like a human 'understanding'.

Searle says that as far as, we can make safe self-driving cars on the roads, who cares if they are conscious or not.

A standard to compare the machine intelligence to humans is the Turing standard, which says if a machine behaves as intelligently as a human being does, then it is as intelligent as a human being is.

Simulating human intelligence will mean that we can define human intelligence systematically, bit-by-bit, precisely. If we can describe every aspect of learning or any other feature of intelligence precisely, step-by-step then it can be simulated in a machine or say computer.

Hubert Dreyfus, an American philosopher says that if the nervous system obeys the laws of physics and chemistry, which we have every reason to suppose it does, then we ought to be able to reproduce the behaviour of the nervous system with some physical device.

We can build the heart circulatory system in a machine because we know how the heart is pumping the blood. However, we do not have any model as to how the brain is producing consciousness, how the neuronal functions in the brain are giving rise to consciousness. Therefore, we are not able to make brain function in a physical device. Not yet.

However, if human consciousness is the artefact of the brain, we will know that optimistically, we will be able to decode it and then a physical device corresponding to the brain will be realizable.

The mind is more than a machine

Gödel's incompleteness theorem demonstrates that the powers of the human mind can outsmart any mechanism. With the human mind, it is always possible to construct a statement that a given consistent formal system of logic could not prove. There can be a formula which machine can not prove to be true but which we can see to be true. Therefore, the power of the human mind is not reducible to a mechanism.

Roger Penrose (1989), an English physicist also holds 'understanding' of a human mind is basically non-computable.

Philosophers Nagel and Newman (1958) and J.R Lucas (1961) also drew the conclusion from incompleteness theorem that mechanism is false and minds cannot be explained as machines.

Philosopher John Searle differentiates between strong AI and weak AI. Strong AI is an artificial intelligence system that has a mind and mental states whereas Weak AI is an artificial intelligence system that can act intelligently.

Artificial intelligence system realized in the physical system always leaves the hard problem of consciousness as envisaged by Philosopher David Chalmers unanswered as to how the matter is generating the subjective experience of perceiving, understanding, or thinking. This hard problem of consciousness is the latest version of the classic mind-body problem.

John Searle argues that actual duplication rather than a simulation of the human brain is required for mental states and consciousness. There are special causal properties of neurons and the actual physical, chemical properties of actual human brains that give rise to minds. There is something special about the configuration and working of the brain that causes mind.

We have advanced in creating artificial intelligent machines to great extents. A robotic creation Sophia who talks, understand human communication and respond to in a human-like manner has been given citizenship rights in Saudi Arabia.

A religion is thought of starting around an artificial intelligent system who would act as God for its followers.

We are talking about creating the artificial organism where the senses and emotional behaviour can be simulated.

Bio-mimetic robots are developing animal capacities in machines.

The day we achieve consciousness in artificial intelligence or say reach singularity as advocated by Ray Kurzweil, we all shall become machines. We shall not need any more concept of soul or God.

However, consciousness concerns those aspects of inner experiences, which are characterized qualitatively in terms of raw feels, what it is like to be, or qualia.

There is still a debate about mechanistic systems. One idea says that the artificial intelligent computer-based machines even in autonomous modes will be limited by its components. They cannot exhibit emotions and free will.

While some others who believe in functionalism like Hillary Putnam (1967) consider, if mental states are defined only in terms of their causal roles then it can be said that any physical system that can instantiate the same pattern of causal roles, will instantiate the same mental states, including consciousness. For functionalists, the mind can be made in computers.

Thought experiment suggest, to know if machines have become conscious

In 1882, Friedrich Nietzsche a German philosopher wrote in a book that 'God is dead'. He considered that the enlightenment brought about by scientific disciplines has killed the possibility of belief in God or gods that ever existed, as he considered the gods to be constructs of humans. In April 1966, Time magazine ran a cover page story 'Is God dead?'

Almost all gods are described in human form.

Gods have been created to show gratitude to nature or out of fear of nature. Many believe God to be omnipotent, omnipresent, and omniscient.

Many people consider that God created the universe and life. In the same manner, many people believe that God was a psychological construct by our ancient ancestors who might have been asking the questions of why and how we are here. What happens after death? Why are we conscious?

Different religions have been created in different cultures, the world over. Religion has been a uniting force in their societies. All religions have some concept of God.

Belief in supernatural powers and entity of God might have provided succour and relief, support and satisfaction to the humans. 'If God exists', is still an open question despite all the advances in the know-how and knowledge produced by science and even today one finds many believers.

Therefore, it can be safely said that the thoughts about the God or supernatural entity had been one of the very first thoughts of the conscious man.

So a thought experiment is suggested to know if the artificial intelligent machines have become conscious or not.

We leave the artificial intelligent machines like Sophia robot, interacting with people around in society and among themselves. If they become conscious any time in future, soon they would realize the importance of the concept of God and belief in God. The day they start believing in God or say they require a God for themselves we should know that these artificially intelligent machines have become conscious. Their mechanistic construct has developed consciousness.

Chapter 16

My personal experience for insight

I had a gradual growth over a period of several years of a lump just adjacent to the elbow tip on my left hand. The lump had grown to three fourth, the size of a table tennis ball and the skin covering the lump was blacky. It was painless and it had become a sort of hard. Its base was large but rounded off on the top. I had shown it to the doctor of medicine. He had told that it would need to be removed by surgical procedure. There was no medicine for it.

I had no problem in arm movement or any of the work. However, it was growing, then, at a faster rate and was a sort of ugly protrusion on the hand.

One day, I prayed, 'hey God! If you are there then cure me of this lump'. I reasoned, at most nothing would happen and it would remain as such on my hand. I also thought that it was not an easy thing and was a difficult thing and it will not be cured. Therefore, in my reasoning, I had set out a difficult thing to happen for God. And a thing, which was not creating much of the trouble for me.

Then I had forgotten that I have made such a testifying prayer for God. Then probably within a week, it might have gone from my hand completely as if nothing was there at the first hand. Even the blackish skin had become skin colour. There was no sign of it. I would rather say no trace of it.

I noticed that this black lump had gone from its place but some smaller growths have developed in my left hand at four-five places and at one-two places in my right hand as if the material of the lump has displaced from its original site and moved at five-six other places beneath the skin. In addition, all the black cells of the lump had perhaps aggregated at one place on my left arm in a mole form. I got these new growths tested and they were found benign growths.

This experience, not only proves that God exists, but also that God knows that he is called by the word God. God also knew that the lump on the elbow was to be cured though I never touched the lump while making the prayer or maybe I have so indicated by touching the lump there while making the prayer. I am not certain.

God knew the best possible way of getting rid of it. He must have known the ins and outs of the body working. He knew that modulating the activity of such and such molecules in the body could correct it. He not only knew but also moved the biomolecules of my body in such a manner that it was completely corrected without any damaging side effects.

Like Descartes, in the darkness of doubts, God was putting the thoughts in his mind to guide him out of darkness or perhaps he, himself, was the author of such thoughts.

Therefore, God acted through my body material while respecting every rule of life and its working. Or perhaps this was possible because the substances, mental substance, as well as body substance of my person had the innate quality of such thing becoming possible.

My prayer was a mind state, a volitional state, a mental state and it moved the matter of my body. The prayer might have been made in the mental state directly or through the brain material but it could move the molecules in my arm in a particular manner. It must have occurred not by the movement of one single molecule but through the movement of a chain of molecules. The mental substance is not only restricted to the brain but also spreads throughout the body.

Therefore, my take away from the experience is that God exists. Mental states affect the body states and the substance, which manifests the mental states, makes the movement of biomolecules. I call it the soul substance. It makes the movement of biomolecules in a sequential and coordinated manner. I have free will down to the levels of biomolecules, which move the biomolecules of my body even out of the way.

This personal experience leads me to make a case for soul substance as an explanation of consciousness.

Chapter 17

Explanation about consciousness in terms of scientific soul substance

One fact perturbs me that even if, in an experiment quite similar to Stanley-Miller experiment, we take DNA, RNA, proteins, carbohydrates, lipids separately and mix them in a pot they do not seem to create life automatically. Some more ingredients are required to start them in a life form.

A popular definition of life as defined by NASA is that life is a self-sustaining chemical system capable of Darwinian evolution.

Brain death people show that they can still be kept alive with mechanical aids even if they are not conscious. Therefore, it seems the condition for being alive is more fundamental than consciousness. Can we search for the reason of the consciousness in the condition of being alive?

Sometimes the concept of being alive is confused with the concept of life.

Parts of a living system may be alive but they do not represent life. Like a cell on my skin is alive but it is not me by any mean. The phrase 'self-sustaining' is used to emphasize that a living system should not need any intervention by some vitalistic force or by a higher entity say 'God' for example and life is just the elaboration of chemistry.

Lawrence Krauss, a theoretical physicist from the USA says that intelligence is an evolutionary imperative. This happens through a series of evolutionary accidents and imperative means that all different routes of evolution lead to more and more intelligence. Evolution causes intelligence to be selected naturally in a way that allows inevitability. If you evolve through different life forms, the intelligent life form will eventually happen and dominate the planet.

Stanford Betty, a philosopher from America, opines that our brain and body is matter and the soul is immaterial because its properties like thoughts and feelings, do not have dimensions. It has no volume, does not have shape, does not have weight but that is real and mind-body dualists say that it is the most important part of us, it is the conscious self, it is the seat of awareness.

Either soul is suffused in the entire body or some say that it is in the pineal gland.

It is the essential self and it is somehow connected with the body and interacts with it continually.

We suppose there is nothing in physics, nothing in science of matter and energy to suggest that consciousness should exist.

How does consciousness jump into existence? Most philosophers, virtually all physicists think there was no such thing at the big bang time, and there was no such thing probably a billion years down the road. Somehow, it emerged and that is one great mystery, science and philosophy are trying to solve. When did it emerge, how did it emerge and does it make any sense to say that it emerged, so there are all kinds of debates go on about this?

In religious tradition like in cabalism, consciousness is part of who we are since the time of conception. It does not emerge out of the brain; the brain is not there yet. There are a material substance and a spiritual substance of the soul; they go together and are created at the same time. One does not emerge out of the other.

Materialism cannot offer any explanation for the field of parapsychology while dualism seems compatible with the empirical data of parapsychology. However, dualists have not been able to offer any good explanation for how the mind and body are able to interact with each other.

A materialist argues that the very fact, damage, or manipulation to the physical brain can result in loss of memories, dramatic personality changes, altered levels of consciousness etc. prove that the mind and brain is one and the same thing.

It is one of the more powerful arguments in the favour of materialism. How the dualism can accommodate this fact?

John Searle says if you knew the actual consciousness producing mechanism, that is, if you knew what caused consciousness in human beings and you knew that something was causally sufficient to cause consciousness then you would be able to produce consciousness in another system.

He sees no obstacle in principle to producing a conscious machine because we are all conscious machines.

Ray Kurzweil, a computer scientist says information processing in the brain happens to run on this biochemical substrate of neurons that generate consciousness and that you could run the same processes on some other substrate like a massively parallel computer, then it can also be conscious. If a non-biological machine passes the Turing test and if we say humans have feelings then it will be easy to assume that non-biological machine also has feelings.

J P Moreland, a philosopher from Biota University in Los Angeles, author of 'Consciousness and the Existence of God', differentiates between a soul which he claims animates all life and consciousness which he says is one of the various faculties of the soul which animals have in differing degrees of complexity. He says that the whole is made of parts in inanimate things and parts came prior like in cars but if whole comes prior to the parts then such things have a soul and are animated life.

All life of any kind, plant or animal, single-cell or multi-cell, have different faculties of consciousness within them.

Kunita and team (2016) showed that paramecium could remember the boundaries of a confined swimming arena. They proposed that the mechanism might be the Ca++ channels located at the anterior of the paramecium.

Even bacteria show life properties and they are affected by common human anaesthetics like isoflurane and sevoflurane, which are volatile anaesthetics and seem to work through their interactions with ion channels. In a study conducted by Mathew Chamberlain and team in 2017, it was found that volatile anaesthetics affected bacterial motility (swimming and gliding) and biofilm formation without any effect on the growth of the common bacterial pathogens.

However, humans can easily be said to be at the pinnacle of consciousness where all faculties of consciousness are functioning optimally.

If biology is simply reducible to chemistry and physics

If biology is essential for the inner experience or we can create consciousness in artificial intelligence systems also, is an enigmatic puzzle, which seeks answers.

If the mind is a completely separate substance from the brain, how can it be possible that whenever the brain is injured, the mind is also changed or compromised?

Our bodies contain trillions of cells and each cell is buzzing around with a whole lot of activities.

Even in seemingly sedentary organisms such as a tree, there happens a lot of motion within their cells.

A living cell environment inside is very dynamic. Life at its most fundamental is a ceaseless concert of motion of biomolecules and the essence of life is in the thousands of chemical reactions involving these biomolecules.

The motion of biomolecules and reactions involving biomolecules within a cell are considered to be a self-sustaining network of chemical reactions.

If we put bacteria, E. coli in a Petri dish with appropriate nutrients, E. coli shows all signs of life and after a few days, the dish will be teeming with new bacterial offsprings.

However, if we break down those same E. coli bacteria into their constituent molecules and keep these molecules in a dish with nutrients it does not show signs of life and nothing further happens.

On the other extreme, dried fertilized eggs from the brine shrimp can be frozen in liquid helium and then, can be slowly warmed to room temperature, hatched and brought to a healthy life again.

This revival of the dried frozen embryo was possible because the spatial arrangement of the biomolecules within the embryo remained intact, which would have kept the chemical pathways preserved.

Therefore, it can be said that life is not simply its constituent molecules but the organization of these molecules within the organism boundaries is equally important. Life is clearly more than the sum of its parts.

The importance of the structural organization of the biomolecules within an organism's system gives us an insight and intuition that it is bound by information hidden within its system. Information in the system should also be about the relative spatial arrangement of these biomolecules that preserves their functionality or say biochemical reaction pathways.

Scientists long ago rejected the idea of a 'life force' giving special properties, say, of self-determination to the living and it is considered an accepted fact that life is just the self-sustaining network of chemical reactions.

Paul Davies, an English physicist from Arizona State University raises big questions-
Do we need new physics to explain life?
Do biological systems hint of what that new physics might be?
The founder of this way of thinking was surely physicist Schrodinger (1944) who in his famous book 'what is life', dealt with the question of the physics of living matter. Schrodinger looked into the question of what is life by considering, "How can the events in space and time which take place within the spatial boundary of a living organism be accounted for by physics and chemistry?"

Erwin Schrodinger physicist has noted the oddity in life. In the case of life, entropy decreases and feeds on negative free energy.

However, he certainly left the question open, in fact, he was inclined to speculate, "Living matter while not eluding the laws of physics as established up to date, is likely to involve other laws of physics hitherto unknown."

In other words, life does not contradict known laws of physics but our existing laws are inadequate to explain all of the apparently magical properties that life has.

This book was written a long time ago. If we take the more recent view, we may consider the opinion of George Whitesides, Harvard chemist about 'if life is just another sort of physical system'. He writes, "How remarkable is life? The answer is: very. Those of us who deal in networks of chemical reactions know of nothing like it."

He is open to the fact that seemingly there is something special and new going on.

In a cell, DNA has 3 billion base pairs, which encode the information about proteins. This is far too much information about cell functioning.

Proteins are made in ribosomes, protein factories which themselves are made of proteins.

There are thousands of chemical reactions happening per second in the cell, which are mediated by very specific enzymes as catalysts, and energy for these reactions are supplied through ATP molecules made in mitochondria.

Proteins are required to be folded in particular shapes and their shapes remain stable inside the cell environment. Outside the cell environment, proteins degrade soon.

Chanelle C. Jumper, a researcher from Canada writes that Living systems are more resistant to perturbations that will normally affect isolated components in vitro. This has been demonstrated long ago that the injection of picric acid into a single-celled amoeba does not coagulate the proteins even at high concentrations as compared to denaturation of proteins in vitro at low concentration of picric acid.

Perhaps, the living systems are more ordered and they have special stabilizing potentials and circuits made out in their physiochemical regime.

Yet processes of life are considered to be understood in term of principles of chemistry and physics. Various processes of life have been well understood in mechanistic terms. Therefore, life does not warrant any need of divine power and is considered abiogenetic in origin.

Life processes as discovered in recent years where it does seem that quantum mechanics is playing a non-trivial role in biology.

All the biology is chemistry and quantum mechanics is helping us to understand chemistry better. When we talk about quantum biology we talk about non-trivial quantum effects like coherence, entanglement, superposition, tunnelling. Quantum aspects of photosynthesis that is in the mainstream chemical analysis have both experimental and theoretical backing.

Nevertheless, human consciousness cannot be due to the quantum phenomenon. One problem is the warm, wet, and noisy environment in the body, which cannot sustain quantum coherence. The other problem is a combination problem as to how Individuated quantum coupling in biological systems can combine to give rise to our coherent stream of consciousness.

We have not made life in the lab nor have got anywhere near doing it. Life is reproduced from life only.

We generally refer to the Miller-Urey experiment in 1952 where the basic building blocks of life amino acids were made rather easily by sparking electricity through a mixture of methane, ammonia and hydrogen gases along with water, thought to represent the atmosphere of the early Earth.

However, if you can get the building blocks of life it does not mean you have made the life, living organism as such.

Making the building blocks is one thing while assembling them into an extraordinarily complex and intricate structure that life represents is quite another.

There was a lot of media hype on the claim of creating life when scientist Craig Venter reprogrammed and reengineered the DNA and put it in the microorganism but it was nothing like assembling living organism from its constituents.

There is little reason to date to think that life may have happened more than once in the observable universe.

Francis Crick has said, "Life on earth seems almost a miracle, so many are the conditions which would have had to have been satisfied for it to get going."

One view is that life is a stupendously improbable accident. It is so complex, so specific in its nature that it would never have happened twice in the observable universe.

Life is a bizarre aberration and extraordinary phenomenon restricted to earth.

However, Christian De Duve, a Nobel prize-winning Belgian biochemist wrote, "life is almost bound to arise wherever physical conditions are similar to earth" and he calls 'life is a cosmic imperative'.

Darwin refused to be drawn on the subject of life's origin. He said, "It is mere rubbish thinking, at present, of the origin of life; one might as well think of the origin of matter."

Explanation in terms of a scientific soul substance

A German author Thomas Mann, in his unfinished 1954 novel 'Confessions of Felix Krull' has said that there are three great mysteries- the creation of matter, life, and consciousness.

However, in my view, there cannot be too many mysteries- one corresponding to consciousness, free will, and self and one for life vitalistics as such. We should somehow see that the mysteries surrounded around life and consciousness can be viewed through one solution.

Here I propose a solution for mysteries around consciousness and life as such in terms of substance dualism wherein I have tried to propose a solution for interaction problem and the structure of the soul itself.

I propose that it is the soul substance, which is causing the biomolecules in the body cells to move. The movement of the biomolecules along the organized pathways are being possible due to this soul substance. The soul substance in the body is making the movement of biomolecules possible in an organized and sequential manner.

Soul substance is a different kind of substance than ordinary matter. In my opinion, it is different from the ordinary matter because it is not affected by gravity yet it contains the information and causes the biomolecules to move. In addition, it has an unlimited capacity to duplicate without losing its capability and information code to cause the biomolecules to move in the cells. It also has the unlimited capacity to merge back from unlimited node points into one single node point without affecting its capability and information code.

Soul substance can be subdivided to sub-cellular cell organelles and yet smaller entities where they are kept alive. The soul substance is synonymous with the 'alive' condition in the form of movement of biomolecules. In fact, it is the very basis of biology.

Once we say what the soul is doing in the body and how it is interacting with the body biomolecules, we can say about the characteristics of the soul.

The soul is causing the biomolecules to move so it is interacting in a manner that it is exchanging force and doing energy exchange with the physical matter of the brain. Therefore, the soul is a substance as it exchanges force and energy and I shall call it soul substance or soul interchangeably.

Movement of the biomolecules is called the essence of life and this movement stops in death.

Soul substance is invisible as during surgery and in labs studying the anatomy of the body, we remain unable to find any trace of it, so the soul substance is also, a very subtle kind of substance but its effect is huge.

Soul substance is extended in space and has its structure made out in a physical matter of the brain and body.

It starts as a node point of the material in the fertilized egg and builds up its life code cell by cell in the form of the whole body.

Thus, soul substance is co-terminus with the extent of the body and the life-code hidden in the soul is made out in the form of cells, tissues, organs, systems and body.

The system-level coding is most obvious in the brain where the soul substance has coded the consciousness, memory in its particular language in the physical matter of neurons.

The life-code of the soul is weaved in the physical material of the cell in the form of DNA, RNA likes and other biomolecules of proteins, fats and carbohydrates and their spatial organisation within the cell.

The material we require from the outside environment is oxygen or air, water and food. As the oxygen is diffused into the blood cells and attaches to haemoglobin making oxy-haemoglobin complex, it becomes part of the biomolecules and becomes under the control of soul substance while carboxy-haemoglobin complex in the biomolecule which is under the control of the soul substance and when it is exhaled in the form of carbon dioxide in lungs it becomes part of the environment. However, inhaling and exhaling process by the expansion and contraction of lungs is under the control of soul substance.

Same is true for the water. Water constitutes 60% of the body mass. This is the solvent in which various biomolecules are dispersed in a cell. And it is because of water that various chemical reactions happening in the body become possible.

The water, which is part of the cell protoplasm, is under the control of soul substance and water taken as a drink, which goes into the stomach, is part of the environment, and the water excreted along with filtered waste material in the kidney again becomes part of the environment.

Food digestion in the gut canal is part of the mechanical process but after absorption through the intestines, it becomes part of body biomolecules under the control of soul substance.

The release of enzymes and acids are the processes carried out by soul substance.

Passage of the food through the gut canal is the mechanistic process but the processes which cause the stomach walls to contract and relax so that the food can be sent down the gut canal, are under the control of soul substance that makes the biomolecules move in the cells and through the combined actions of the cells, the stomach walls are moved in a mechanistic manner to make the food pass through the gut canal and digesting and absorbing the food through the intestinal walls as it passes through the gut canal.

Soul substance starts as a node point coterminous with the fertilized egg and as the cell divides, the soul substance also gets extended to this new cell in the process of division itself. In the human body through each cell is self-sufficient but remain interconnected and make tissues and organs. Similarly, the node point of the soul substance also is extended to this new cell but soul substance is not separated out from the parent node point and remains connected. In the case of unicellular organism, as the cell divides and reproduces the new unicellular organism, the new node point of the soul substance is separated out from the parent node point of the soul substance.

In case of wounds or injury, along with the body cells, the soul substance also is severed. Here it shrinks its soul substance to the nearby live region of the wounds. As the wound is healed, the extension of the soul substance happens along with the growth of body cells, at the site of the wound.

In death, different organs of the body remain alive for different periods. As more and more cells of the body dies that means the molecular motion in the cells come to a stop, the extension of the soul in this area shrinks to the remaining alive region and on full death of the body the whole extension of the node reduces to one node point only.

This node point does not have its independent existence, rather upon death, the node point soul substance merges with other nodes (extended nodes of living organisms), mainly to the nodes of family members or of near and dear ones. The node points of soul substance upon death merge with the living node of family members or near and dear ones, even if these living nodes are not in the vicinity but are distant or these may also merge with the living nodes of the vicinity or distant, at random.

However, in cases of amputation etc., more than one node points may be generated from the single extended node but then these extra node points merge with other extended nodes of soul substance.

These node points of soul substances are the information and knowledge-based node points so they may seek out the merger with specific nodes of family members even if they are at a distance and not in the vicinity.

Now, as the soul substance exchanges energy with the physical matter, it is pertinent to think about what could be its energy source. We find the clue in the fact that, with the decrease of every ten degrees in the temperature of the body, the metabolism of the body is reduced to its half speed.

With the decrease in temperature, not only the rate of the chemical reaction is reduced but also the speed of movement of the biomolecule is reduced.

Therefore, I propose that the soul substance derives its energy from the thermal vibrations of the molecules and channelize it in the movement of the biomolecules. With the decrease in temperature, the thermal vibrations reduce and so the energy given by the soul substance to channelize the physical matter is also reduced which reduces the speed of the movement of biomolecules.

Based on this formulation for the nature of the soul substance and its interaction with the physical matter, we may look into the observed phenomenon of life and consciousness and we may look if they would be able to explain the phenomenon of consciousness, free will, self, and subjective or first-person availability of the experience.

Phenomenal qualities of seeing, hearing, smell, taste, and touch are basically the qualities of the soul substance. It is because of the soul substance, one has mental qualities of feelings and pain. Seeing of colours is due to the phenomenal property of the soul substance.

Soul has its structure as same as the structure of the cells, tissues, organs, systems and body. The structure of the soul is as elaborate as the structure of the brain and body. Therefore, the different phenomenal qualities like hearing, seeing, smelling, taste and touch can all appear as the distinct qualities of the same soul.

Soul substance is co-terminus with the body. It is the quality of the soul substance to have an experience. Therefore, the experience would be known to the person having the experience. It will not be known outside of this soul substance. This explains the first person availability of the experience. Experiences will have subjectivity about them. Thus, this explains the hard problem of consciousness as framed by David Chalmers.

The states of soul substance will be the mental states while the states of the physical matter like the brain are the matter states. Because the soul and the physical states of body and brain are in continuous interaction so it would be possible mental states affecting the physical states and physical states affecting the mental states of the person.

The soul can have an independent mental thought to do a certain thing such as moving his hand, which in turn would influence the physical state of the brain and body and the person moves his hand. Thus, in this soul-body model of life, the individual has the free will at the very basic. He not only has the free will but also the strong sense of having free will. This free will extends up to the biomolecules level and it makes it possible to affect the various metabolic pathways in the life-chemistry say by the use of medicines.

Soul has the undivided continuum extended throughout the body even when the old cells die and new cells are replenished. So the soul continuity maintained as bodily continuity. So the self and the experience of self can be said is due to the soul continuity of the soul and is more basic and can be the basis of personal identity and feeling of 'I' or 'me'. This soul is the agency for 'self' and free will.

Since one has the conscious experience of seeing as if the viewer is sitting right behind the retina so that he sees the objects of the world as being projected out there in the world at the same place and distance. As in this model of soul-body, soul substance is in continuum presence from the retina to cortex so the phenomenal quality of seeing can be operated from as if the viewer is right behind the retina.

Similarly, pain is felt at the location of injury rather than in the brain. The sensation of touch is felt at the location of the touch. These may be the property of the soul-body interface that the phenomenal property is located at the site of origin. The soul acts as the decoder of the coded language of physical states of the brain and body and expresses them as phenomenal experiences.

In this model of the soul-body duality, because the soul has the same structure as the brain so the binding factor could be the soul itself or the unified phenomenal quality of subjective experience may itself be first getting realized in brain structures and then getting expressed in the soul.

Soul structure is the same as that of the brain and body. Therefore, mind and brain are so intimately connected that every time there is damage to the brain, the mind gets affected.

The soul is having its own information channels, which are getting realized through the information made out in the physical matter. Similarly, the memory requirements of the soul should also be getting realized through the physical matter.

However, in certain circumstances, soul phenomenal qualities and memory qualities may be getting expressed as loosened with the physical states of the brain as happens in the cases of NDE. Later on, these experiences having phenomenal qualities and memory may be made realized in the physical matter of the brain also so that it may be recalled as the person returns back to conscious states.

Upon death, the node point merges with the node of living family members or near and dear ones, so it can be the reason that in NDE the person sometimes experiences meeting with his dead relatives.

Seeing of phenomenal screen or mind screen as happens in case of visualization, imagery, dreams and hallucinations can also be explained as the phenomenal quality of the soul getting expressed when the physical states of the brain matter are affected in a certain manner say by exerting the brain states intentionally as in visualization, imagery or spontaneously as in dreams or by use of drugs as in hallucinations.

Upon death, the node point can merge with the living nodes at vicinity or distant nodes at random also so sometimes we find the examples of memory recall of a dead person by some children, so-called reincarnations. The node point of the dead person who met a sudden death may carry the memories of the dead person because the soul substance has the qualities of memory also in it, which may be getting expressed in such cases.

Thus, we see that by formulating the soul-body dualistic model this way, I am able to show the interaction of soul substance and physical matter of the brain and body as well as the structure of the soul.

It is able to explain free will, experiences of seeing, hearing and likes. It is able to explain 'self', the experience of 'I' as the whole body expression and not only the brain. It also explains why the feeling of pain or touch happens at the place of cause.

It is able to explain the phenomenal qualities of conscious experience as well as the phenomenal screen in case of dreams etc. as the innate qualities of the soul. Qualia are the characteristic of the soul substance.

It is able to explain the subjectivity and first-person availability of the conscious experience. Thus, it explains the hard problem of consciousness.

It offers an explanation for NDE and reincarnations. In the next chapter, we see that such formulation offers an explanation for the origin of life also.

Chapter 18

The origin of life explanation

Darwinian Evolutionary theory holds that human evolution in its present form has happened via gradual events where natural selection was superimposed upon random variation. Natural selection from among the varied offspring has given the direction to evolutionary process on earth.

The genetic mutations are random as we see some mutations that make some children sick. Some mutations can be fatal also as we see in cancer patients. If it was not natural and random and would have been happening due to some higher reason say by intelligence selection then there should not have occurred harmful mutations in DNA.

Darwin's theory of biological evolution suggests that all diverse forms of life on earth, for example, plants, animals, bacteria, fungi including us humans have evolved from the last universal common ancestor that was of reproducing kind living in the distant past. All living cells have DNA, RNA, energy-producing mechanism, metabolism, cell membranes and the studies of DNA, RNA and proteins of all known present-day species indicate that all life has many similarities and should have, in fact, evolved from the earliest form of simple primitive reproducing lifeform.

Earth has formed in our solar system about 4.54 billion years ago and oceans have formed about 4.4 billion years ago. Earliest known fossils in rocky aggregates in Australia, so-called stromatolites, date back to 3.5 billion years. However even these fossil organisms were quite complex lifeforms and they cannot have been the most primitive lifeforms. In 2017, possibly the oldest forms of fossilized microorganisms have been reported in hydrothermal vents in Quebec, Canada that date back to 4.28 billion years old.

Therefore, it seems, life emerged soon after the oceans formed. According to the opinion of biologist Stephen Blair Hedges, "If life arose relatively quickly on Earth ... then it could be common in the universe."

Our studies of reproducing cells tell that their interior machinery of biomolecules is too complex to have evolved into existence in a single step. Moreover, evolution would have required reproduction to work.

Evolution does not explain the origin of life, which needs its own explanation.

Life is thought to be originated from pre-life chemical reactions

Life is explained as a network of self-sustaining chemical reactions that enable an organism to repair and reproduce in such a way that the continued functionality of the system as a whole is maintained throughout.

In the scientific era, it is presumed that the origin of life on earth happened through a natural process and no divine intervention is required to set the life on the path of evolution.

Life on earth or the biochemistry that made the first replicating life forms has generated from pre-life chemical reactions.

Darwin wrote in 1863 that at those times it was premature to think about as to how the first life came to be in existence. One might as well talked about how the matter could have come to exist.

In 1871, Darwin wrote his opinion about the possible origin of life, "But if (and oh what a big if) we could conceive in some warm little pond with all sorts of ammonia & phosphoric salts,— light, heat, electricity etc. present, that a protein compound was chemically formed, ready to undergo still more complex changes..."

The modern theory is the abiogenesis theory that life has arisen from non-living matter such as simple organic compounds through a gradual natural process. The framework of the chemical evolution of life was laid out by Oparin (1924) and Haldane (1925).

They theorized that early earth had a chemically reducing atmosphere. Organic molecules like amino acids could be created from non-living molecules in an oxygenless atmosphere through the action of sunlight. These organic molecules accumulated in a primordial soup where they combined in complex ways and made complex organic polymers.

Some of these oily chemicals formed spherical globules, called coacervate droplets. These droplets can fuse together to grow and subdivide into daughter droplets. They would have provided an enclosure for lifelike chemicals and that would have been a starting point for life.

This theory of the origin of life through chemical reactions got a boost by Stanley- Miller experiment in 1953 where amino acids were produced by simple chemistry of methane, ammonia, hydrogen, and water vapour. The required energy for chemical reactions was provided by electrical sparks.

Many other experiments done in the later years have shown that different organic building blocks like amino acids, sugars, lipids and others can form from inorganic molecules.

Researchers have recently discovered that meteorites that are rocks fallen to earth from outer space, contained many of the molecules like amino acids and sugars that are building blocks of life before they fell on the earth. This tells us that these special carbon-based compounds can be produced spontaneously in conditions existing in space.

Therefore, it seems reasonable to think that precursor organic molecules of life would have been present on the early earth.

Many of the life-creating molecules and cellular reactions are possible to be recreated in lab suggesting that life is powered by normal chemical reactions and no vital force or biotic energy is required to sustain life.

Then it becomes natural to think that life itself may have emerged from non-living pre-life chemistry.

The transition from non-living matter such as simple organic compounds to living life would have been a gradual natural process, which increased in complexity in its formation, interaction, and organisation of the biomolecules.

Although, the emergence of life from non-living pre-life chemical reactions is generally undisputed among scientists, there are different hypotheses supported by different scientists based on the researches done by these scientists to explain the origin of life.

Some scientists advocate the RNA first hypothesis where there could have been an RNA, which could be self-replicating as well as worked as a catalyst. This RNA could have been in a membranous like enclosure, which could have been the starting point of life.

Other scientists favour the metabolism first hypothesis where some kind of ionic gradients in geological formations could have sustained the metabolic networks before DNA or RNA.

Why life is not created in the present

Why life does not originate now, in spite of much more hospitable conditions and presence of all kinds of organic, inorganic molecules is a moot question. Darwin explains, "At the present day such matter would be instantly devoured or absorbed which would not have been the case before living creatures were formed."

Oparin in 1924 while proposing the chemical origin of life reasoned that presently, the atmospheric oxygen would have been preventing the synthesis of certain organic compounds that might be the necessary building blocks for life.

Why not Intelligent design theory

Many religions invoke the intervention of the divine in creating life. These theories consider that God breathed life into matter. Such a theory requiring the intervention of God is called Creationism or intelligent design theory. However, such intervention by God negates the evolutionary theory of life progress.

If we consider it to be a one-time intervention of God in just creating the life then also it seems unreasonable as to why and where the presence of such an all-powerful, almighty God has got lost during subsequent times.

Life is created from life only

Until the 19th century, there had been a belief in spontaneous generation of life where the people generally saw that living organisms were getting generated from the decaying organic matter.

William Harvey (1578-1657), an English physician, who had explained the human circulatory system of blood in detail proposed that all life began from an egg. Francesco Redi, an Italian physician, demonstrated (1668) that maggots in putrefying meat had come from the eggs of flies and thus challenged the theory of spontaneous generation.

Still many believers in a spontaneous generation used to claim that microbes could arise spontaneously.

In 1745, John Needham, an English biologist did the experiments where he boiled the chicken broth in a flask and then left it open to cool. It was found that microbes grew in the flask. He proposed these experiments as proof of spontaneous generation.

But, maybe the boiling time was insufficient to have killed all microbes and open flask could have caused microbial contamination.

In 1768, Lazzaro Spallanzani, an Italian scientist sealed the flask after boiling the broth for sufficient time. No microbes were grown in the flask.

However, it was the series of experiments by Louis Pasteur (1861), a French biologist that disproved the doctrine of spontaneous generation conclusively. He demonstrated in his experiments that even microbes such as bacteria and fungi are not spontaneously created in a sterile but nutrient-rich medium without contamination.

His experiments have proved the theory of biogenesis that all living things come from pre-existing living things only, by means of reproduction. Cell theory of biology, which is a universally accepted scientific theory states that cells are the basic structural and functional unit of life and cells are reproduced from the cells only.

Discontinuity is a flaw

The modern theory of the origin of life is the theory that life was created from non-living pre-biotic chemistry. Thus, it presents a discontinuity at the instant of creation of life. Principle of biogenesis breaks down if we consider that life originated on earth from non-living matter through the pre-life chemical reactions.

In my opinion, this discontinuity is a major flaw and this discontinuity should be one of the major obstacles in accepting the purely chemical evolution of life from non-living substances.

In my theory of soul substance giving movement to life creating biomolecules, such a discontinuity is naturally avoided.

Possibility of life elsewhere also

Nevertheless, if life on earth is just the chemical reactions and originated from pre-life chemical reactions then there is a good possibility that life would have started in, at least, few of the trillions of planets of billions of stars in each one of billions of galaxies.

We can detect the presence of life at other planets from the biological signatures present in their atmospheric spectrum or from the signature of intelligence through the radio astronomy.

Although the search for extraterrestrial life is going on, the earlier hints are that earth is a very special place that bears life and is just fine-tuned for life.

Information in DNA

Life in a cell is very complex and DNA is the coded information, which carries the blueprint of life. Therefore, the argument goes that information in such a condensed form cannot just arise spontaneously and supernatural powers must be involved and this is intelligent design.

Researchers are yet to show, how through the geochemical non-living world, the replicating life would have emerged. However, they are progressing through a step-by-step approach, yet huge explanting gap persists.

Life is carbon-based and water is essential. There are four key families of chemicals, which build the life- lipids (cell membrane), carbohydrates (sugars, cellulose), amino acids (proteins), and nucleic acids (DNA and RNA). The origin of life theory should be able to explain the origins and interactions of these groups of molecules.

Explanation of origin of life, based on soul substance formulation

As I have envisaged of a soul substance in the last chapter that makes the biomolecules move and it is the magic soup of life. In this chapter, it is explained that this soul substance was responsible for originating the life here on earth.

Soul substance was present in node point form and the conditions on the earth were amenable to the emergence of life. Either the organic molecules were present which could have been required to start life or even these materials were arranged by the soul substance to make from the precursor molecules. These precursor molecules and biomolecules were set into moving by the soul substance in a particular sequential manner up to the point when the first self-replicating living cell and no less than a self-replicating cell came into existence to kick start life. One node point of the soul substance created just one self-replicating cell.

Now, this self-replicating living cell kept on replicating itself and thus extending the movement of molecules from one node to another node, that is, from this original living cell, many other duplicating living cells were created which further created the self-replicating living cells. And the process of life and evolution started on earth.

The universe started as Big Bang. This soul substance was present as a node point at the time of the big bang. After the big bang, material produced was in the form of hydrogen and helium. From this material, early stars were formed. Moreover, when these stars died in the form of the supernova explosion, the heavier elements of periodic table like C, N, O, P would have formed.

From these heavier elements, an earth-like planet in our solar system would have formed. The node point of soul substance would have kept on hitchhiking from one place to another during the formation process of the universe and would have been present in a node point form at one of such places. This node point of soul substance came to be present in our solar system and now we know that node point was luckily stuck at the earth planet.

On earth, as the conditions for the emergence of life became stable and hospitable, this node point of soul substance would have caused the assemblage of biomolecules and eventually the self-replicating life.

The life code for self-replicating life was always there in this node point of soul substance. The situation is quite like a seed of life, which kept on hitchhiking during the process of formation of the universe and ultimately settled on earth where it found the conditions amenable for germination of life and life started here on earth as the first original self-replicating cell germinated from this node point of soul substance.

Here I stop short of saying that since the very beginning of big bang the node point of soul substance had worked in a manner to create the conditions at one of the places required called Earth to kick start self-replicating life form.

Soul substance would have been putting the molecules into a coordinated movement. This would have acted as a selection of molecules as only those molecules could have been selected which would have been possible to be moved in consonance with the already moving molecular machine. This can be an explanation for the selection of chirality or handedness in the making of life.

As there was only one node point of soul substance, which had the code to start life quite like a seed, since the beginning of the universe and it settled on earth and when the conditions on earth became hospitable and life got started in the form of one original self-replicating cell. Therefore, it can be said that life originated on earth only. There can be no other place in the universe where life can be found.

There was only one node point of the soul substance and that created the first original replicating cell on earth. Therefore, life started on the earth only once in the form of one original self-replicating cell. There cannot be a second chance when life could have started on earth.

Information in the condensed form about the code of starting life and continuing and maintaining it was carried by this node point. So life started as a replicating cell and no less, as the soul substance carried the life code of a replicating cell.

At the death, the node point merges with another node. At the end of life on earth, there will still be left one node point, which will carry the code of life. This node point may further find its journey to another hospitable part of the universe, after say 4.5 billion years- the estimated life of the earth. Thus in a way life is eternal in the form of node point of soul substance.

Paul Davies, an English physicist, says that there can be that life started on earth itself, not once but many times, in many forms. For example, life, as we know, is based on left-handed amino acids and right-handed sugars, but we may find a lifeform with opposite kinds, a mirror lifeform, that is, right-handed amino acids and left-handed sugars then we can say that life started not once but twice.

If we ever find any other life at any other planet, other than earth through our attempts like SETI or through the chemical signatures in the planet's atmospheric spectrum or we ever find the second chance of a life happening here itself on earth as suggested by Paul Davies, then the whole theory built up along the lines in this book about soul and God will need to be evaluated again, as it would mean that life is a cosmic imperative and happens from chemistry.

Chapter 19

Parapsychology and interconnected consciousness

Somehow it seems to be odd and incomplete if we leave the living nodes of soul substances rolling here and there on the planet earth independent of each other without any connection whatsoever between them. So I think some method of interconnection between the nodes should be there.

Indication of interconnected consciousness in parapsychology

Interconnectedness is also indicated in the data collected in the labs of parapsychology researchers like Charles Tart, Russell Targ, and Marilyn Schlitz.

It is commonly felt if somebody stares at a person intensely and even if this person was facing in the opposite direction, he gets a feel that somebody is needing his attention and he looks back. Maybe some parapsychological communication happens.

This psychic staring effect feeling has also been investigated in lab settings by Rupert Sheldrake.

So here, the method and possible rules of interconnected consciousness are postulated.

The first rule of interconnected consciousness

As we have seen that a probe into the question of consciousness, the subjective experience the person has, leads us to stipulate the soul substance, which is co-terminus with the body. This soul substance makes possible the movement of biomolecules that go into making the cell, in a sequential and purposeful way of making the cell 'alive'.

Each living organism acts as a node of soul substance. These nodes are free to move places and are independent of one another. However, these nodes are also interconnected in a way. The mode of interconnection between them can be understood if we take the example of nodes which humans inhabit.

It is proposed that when a person (one node) thinks about other person (other node) then a very minuscule part, a consciousness factor called here 'ε' (epsilon) transmits from this person to other person. Other node may be present in the vicinity or maybe at a distant place. These nodes as well as the consciousness factors 'ε' are identifiable by the personal characteristic of the person like name, relations etc. as these nodes are the nodes of information and knowledge.

For example, when a person thinks about his family members or friends or celebrities etc. then the minuscule consciousness factor ε transmits from this person to the other person about whom he thinks. Here it is implicit that if a person is talking about a person he is thinking about that person.

Thus, there keeps on happening the transmission of 'ε' consciousness factors among the nodes humans inhabit.

It is also proposed that soul substance, a node in each organism, is having the same basic characteristic except that soul substance has weaved more and more evolved consciousness and free will through the process of evolution in the physical matter of the organisms. Therefore, the transmission of 'ε' consciousness factor is possible across all nodes of all organisms.

However, as mostly, human thoughts will be about other humans so the transmission of consciousness factors from humans will be mostly among the nodes humans inhabit and the thoughts of monkeys may be about other monkeys so the transmission of 'ε' factors will mostly be among the nodes, which monkeys inhabit.

Therefore, in my view, there can be said to be two rules to govern the process of exchange of these consciousness factors ε.

The first rule is that the soul substances in all nodes are independent of one another but they remain interconnected through the exchange of a very minuscule conscious factor ε among one another. When a person (organism) thinks about another person (organism) while thinking includes if a person (one node) is talking name of other person (other node) he is thinking about that person, a minuscule consciousness factor ε transfers from one node to other node.

The second rule of interconnected consciousness

As we see a natural tendency among humans to yearn for recognition. In a way, he yearns to increase his consciousness by being a thought centre to many so that he can receive more numbers of 'ε' consciousness factors.

Therefore, in humans, we see a pattern that every person tries to maximize his consciousness by increasing his receiving of ε consciousness factors. This leads me to the second rule of consciousness.

The second rule is that each organism tries to maximize his consciousness by maximizing its receiving more of ε consciousness factors.

Conclusion

Stipulating interconnections among these nodes (extensions of node points) through the exchange of minuscule consciousness factors 'ε' give us a possibility that parapsychological phenomenon may happen. Moreover, who knows such things are detectable also as Dean Radin experiments claim to show.

www.ingramcontent.com/pod-product-compliance
Lightning Source LLC
LaVergne TN
LVHW041311200726